Crash Course in Reference

Recent Titles in
Libraries Unlimited Crash Course Series

Crash Course in Reference

Charlotte Ford

Crash Course

LIBRARIES

U N L I M I T E D

A Member of the Greenwood Publishing Group

Westport, Connecticut • London

Library of Congress Cataloging-in-Publication Data

Ford, Charlotte.
   Crash course in reference / Charlotte Ford.
       p. cm. — (Crash course)
   Includes bibliographical references and index.
   ISBN 978–1–59158–463–6 (alk. paper)
  1. Reference services (Libraries)—Handbooks, manuals, etc.
I. Title.
 Z711.F645 2008
 025.5'2—dc22   2007052948

British Library Cataloguing in Publication Data is available.

Library of Congress Catalog Card Number: 2007052948
ISBN: 978–1–59158–463–6

First published in 2008

Libraries Unlimited, 88 Post Road West, Westport, CT 06881
A Member of the Greenwood Publishing Group, Inc.
www.lu.com

Printed in the United States of America

The paper used in this book complies with the
Permanent Paper Standard issued by the National
Information Standards Organization (Z39.48–1984).

10 9 8 7 6 5 4 3 2 1

CONTENTS

PREFACE

This crash course is written for the "practicing librarian" working in a small public library—for that dedicated individual whose life path may not have presented an opportunity to acquire an academic degree in Library & Information Science, but who is eager to understand more about librarianship and wishes to master the skills it takes to provide excellent library service. Reading this book is not the same as completing a graduate course in Library & Information Science, but it will give you the opportunity to learn about reference service and introduce you to some of the basic reference sources that are available to you and your patrons.

There are many challenges involved in working in a small library. You could probably use some more money to spend on books and CDs and DVDs and computer technology; it would be terrific to have more staff to help you out; and wouldn't it be wonderful if you were paid a bit more as well? But despite the challenges involved, library work can also be quite rewarding.

People value their libraries greatly. They say things like:

I love to read. I think the library is a great thing for kids to have for their imaginations, and be able, whether you're rich or poor, or whatever, to have an escape.[1]

The library here is a meeting space, it's readily accessible, it's an attractive, well-kept space, it's full of activities, book sales, exhibits and things like that. It's really great.[2]

I love the library! All that knowledge in one place.[3]

A library is vital in order to get information. I trust and love libraries. The web cannot take over because the library is sacred.[4]

Although small, this library is a lifeline to a community and a larger body of contemporary thinking, ideas, and research.[5]

You must value libraries as well—or presumably, you wouldn't be working in one! If you are in a small setting, you may be "the face of the library"—a person who does everything, from unlocking the door, to purchasing books, to greeting people as they come by, to reshelving materials at the end of the day. Providing high-quality, personalized reference service is yet another way of adding value to an institution that is there to serve the general public and help people make their way through everyday life.

NOTES

1. Public Agenda Foundation, Americans for Libraries Council, & Bill & Melinda Gates Foundation. (2006). *Long overdue: A fresh look at public attitudes about libraries in the 21st century.* New York: Public Agenda. Available at http://www.lff.org/long_overdue061306.html.
2. ibid.
3. Online Computer Library Center (2005). *Perceptions of libraries and information resources.* Dublin, OH: OCLC. Available at http://www.oclc.org/reports/2005perceptions.htm.
4. ibid.
5. Vavrek, B. (1990). *Assessing the information needs of rural Americans.* Clarion, PA: College of Library Science, Center for the Study of Rural Librarianship, Clarion University of Pennsylvania, p. 12.

ACKNOWLEDGMENTS

I would like to acknowledge the support and encouragement of my editor, Blanche Woolls, who had faith in my ability to produce this book. Jeffrey Karlsen, research assistant *extraordinaire,* has been tremendous; he has had a hand in every chapter of the book, and deserves more thanks than I can possibly give. Kate Lippincott and Mary C. Bushing provided helpful comments on the manuscript, on very short notice. Raymundo Andrade played a key role in developing the index. My friends and family, as always, have been patient and supportive. And finally, a special thanks to my students— for pushing me to learn new things.

RUSA Guidelines for Behavioral Performance of Reference and Information Service Providers (http://www.ala.org/ala/rusa/protools/referenceguide/guidelinesbehavioral.cfm), excerpted extensively on p.17, © Copyright 2004, American Library Association; Code of Ethics of the American Library Association (http://www.ala.org/ala/oif/statementspols/codeofethics/codeethics.htm), reproduced on pp.102–3, © Copyright 1997, American Library Association.

CHAPTER 1

What Is Reference Service?

*A hearty reception by a sympathizing friend, and the recognition of some
one at hand who will listen to inquiries, even although he may consider them
unimportant, make it easy for such persons to ask questions, and put them at
once on home footing.*[1]

So wrote Samuel S. Green, the father of modern reference service (and a librarian
at the Worcester Free Public Library in Massachusetts) in 1876. The basic idea of a
friendly and sympathetic person, who is willing to listen to someone's questions and
help them find answers, is still at the heart of reference service today, 130 years later.
When we think of reference service, we think first and foremost of the personal touch
of the librarian who accompanies a patron in his or her search for information.

A good working definition of reference service (offered by the American Library
Association back in 1990) is the "personal assistance provided to users and potential
users of information."[2] Naturally, this service involves using the library's resources to
help answer the questions that patrons may pose in person, over the phone, or over the
computer. In addition, reference service may include activities such as guiding patrons
in their selection of books (also known as readers' advisory), helping students figure
out how to get started on a term paper, and offering general instruction in the use of the
library and its resources.[3]

WHAT IS A REFERENCE QUESTION?

People come to the library with different needs. They may be looking for leisure reading, for romances or mysteries or adventure books. They may have more practical goals in mind: how to fix a broken bicycle, how to make a special dessert, how to find information for a school report. They may want to check out a movie or casually surf the Web. Or they may just need to get out of the house for awhile, to attend a book discussion group or simply to see a few friendly, familiar faces.

For all of these needs, the librarian is there to help.

Here are a few of the questions recently overheard at a local public library, over the course of a few hours:

> Where's the bathroom?
> What are your hours?
> Can you help me make a photocopy?
> My computer has frozen up!
> Where are your newspapers?
> I got this number—how do I find the books?

> I'm looking for books by Franz Kafka.
> I need travel books about Alaska.
> Do you have *The Double Life of Pocahontas*?
> My daughter is looking for books on colleges.

> I need a phone number for someone in Valley Station, Kentucky. I have the name
>   and address but no phone number.
> Which boils faster, salt water or tap water?
> Do you know what forms I use for taxes? I've worked out of state.

> I need information on cat's claw, the herbal supplement.
> I'd like to see a Web site on jobs.
> I have to write a paper on pollution in a city such as Los Angeles. I looked on the
>   Internet and I couldn't find anything!

Several things about this list of questions are worth noting. First, not all of these are posed as classic "questions," ending with a question mark; there are also needs, wishes, and even exclamations. ("My computer has frozen up!" "I looked on the Internet and I couldn't find anything!") The librarian must always listen carefully to understand what the patron is trying to communicate.

Second, some of these questions are more difficult than others. The first six questions are directional; the patrons are simply asking librarians to direct them to a location or are asking for help in using technology. The second set of questions requires knowledge of how to use the catalog effectively to look for books; the third set may require the use of specific reference sources; and the last three questions will probably require some in-depth research and involve using a variety of library sources. As we all know, anyone who's been working in a library building more than a few minutes can probably direct a patron to the bathroom; it may take a bit more work to help someone find travel books on Alaska, and it will be even more of a challenge to help someone find the correct tax forms to use. Chapters 4 through 9 introduce some of the basic reference sources and search techniques to better assist patrons.

Third, to answer some of the questions, specifically, those near the end of the list, you may have to talk with the patron for awhile to figure out what the user really needs and what kind of information would help him or her the most. In the lingo of librarianship, this is known as "the reference interview." Some questions are straightforward and direct, but others are not, and sometimes people hesitate to express exactly what they need or may not be able to express their needs easily. In such cases, a bit of back-and-forth dialog with the patron may be required. We address the topic of the reference interview in Chapter 2.

By the end of this "crash course," I hope that you will recognize when you might need to interview patrons who have more complex questions (and know how to do so without stepping on their toes), and that you will feel comfortable using catalogs, databases, and other kinds of reference sources (both print and electronic) to help patrons find answers to their questions. Have no fear! Chances are, you already possess much of the knowledge it takes to provide outstanding reference service, or as Dr. Spock said in his classic reference book on *Baby and Childcare,* "You know more than you think you do."

WHAT DOES IT MEAN TO PROVIDE REFERENCE SERVICE?

Several years ago, I spent many hours hanging out in a public library watching reference librarians and patrons interact (one of my favorite things to do). Afterwards, I sat down and systematically analyzed exactly what reference librarians do at work. This is what I came up with:

1.   Reference librarians *communicate* (with patrons and with each other).
2.   Reference librarians *search* (using many different tools, print and electronic).
3.   Reference librarians *evaluate* (sources, patrons, and their own abilities to answer questions).
4.   Like it or not, reference librarians *troubleshoot technology* (not just computer technology, but also things like copy machines and library shelving systems).

When you provide reference service, you will be doing all four of these things. You may not be doing all of them with every patron who comes to the door, but at different moments during your workday, each of these activities will probably come into play. Let's look at each one in turn.

Communication

Communicating with patrons is the most obvious part of reference work. A patron walks into the library, or telephones, or e-mails with a question of some sort, and as a librarian, your job is to respond to this request. Your responses might include simple directions (to the magazines, to the bathroom) or quick referrals (to the mayor's office), or they might involve giving the patron a call number area in which, for instance, the books on horses might be found.

But often communication is much more than this. Librarians also explain complex information, such as how to understand the ratings given in *Consumer Reports* or how to read a table in the *Statistical Abstract*. Instead of just giving a call number, you might walk with a patron to the shelves and help him or her find a book. Instead of waiting for a patron to approach the desk with a question, you can reach out with a greeting and an offer of assistance: "How may I help you?" Good, caring librarians reach out to their patrons and often give them more than they ask for. For instance, if someone asks where the books on choosing a college are, you might (in addition to showing him or her books) point out the books on college scholarships and offer to help locate some Internet resources on choosing a college as well.

Reference work often has teaching aspects such as showing patrons how to search the catalog, how to use databases, and how to work the copy machine. Whether consulting the printed index of a book or searching the Internet for an obscure bit of information, good librarians often model and explain the *process* they go through to find information.

An important part of the communication process involves simply talking with patrons, chatting or joking with them, and sometimes reassuring them. It can be intimidating for people to ask questions of a librarian; some people see this as an admission of ignorance, and it makes them feel quite vulnerable. People often start their questions like this:

"This is probably a stupid question, but . . . "
"I'm sorry to bother you, but . . . "
"This is my first time in this library . . . "

When this happens, the best tactic is to say something that will put the patron at ease. In response to the first comment, for instance, you might smile and remark, "There are no stupid questions!" I have also heard a librarian say, with a twinkle in her eye, "Stupid questions are my *very* favorite kind!" It's important to let your patrons know that you care about them, respect their intelligence, and welcome their questions. These interpersonal aspects are a key part of successful reference work.

Finally, communication with other librarians also forms an important part of reference work. In a small library, you may be the only person on the staff; fortunately, thanks to the telephone and the Internet, you are not alone! Friends and colleagues in your local area, your state, or the country are never far away and can be called on as needed.

Searching

In addition to communicating, reference work involves a great deal of searching. If you have an innate sense of curiosity, or enjoy a good mystery story, or like working puzzles, chances are you will have a lot of fun providing reference service. In doing reference work, you will find yourself searching many different tools: the library catalog, online databases, print reference books, Internet search engines, specific sources on the Web, your own personal files, and so on. This means familiarizing yourself with many different sources and knowing how to find the information contained in them (using tables of contents, indexes, and of course search commands). It also means being intimately familiar with every nook and cranny of your library and having a good general sense of what is in your collection (both reference and circulating items).

The best reference librarians are *tenacious* in their searching: they take a personal interest in people's questions and sometimes find it hard to let go of them. They play with different search terms and strategies and try different sources if they are not happy with their results, at times drawing on different sources to piece together an answer, or comparing what different sources have to say. They are not afraid to talk with the patron as they work toward an answer and don't hesitate to call on friends and colleagues for ideas and suggestions when they feel stumped. And if they reach a point where they've done all they can and still haven't found a good answer, then they try to refer the patron to other appropriate libraries or resources.

If you work in a library that serves a small community, you may already have a couple of advantages that will help you build your search skills. First, you probably know many of your patrons and already feel a personal connection with them and their questions, which is a great motivator for being a persistent searcher. Second, it's likely that you are familiar with local resources and know people you can count on and call upon. Personal knowledge of the patrons, the library, and your community are all extremely useful when it comes to searching for answers.

Evaluation

Evaluation is another important part of reference service. When doing reference work, you must constantly evaluate sources, the needs of your patrons, and your own abilities. Particularly in a small community, a librarian is seen as an *authority*, as someone who can provide definitive answers to questions like how to find "legitimate" information on herbal supplements, or how the different nationalities came about. Patrons place a lot of confidence in your judgment of sources, and thus you have a responsibility to evaluate sources carefully *and* to explain the process of evaluation to your patrons.

As you assist your patrons, you will almost automatically find yourself evaluating them as well, asking yourself questions like: "Can this young man find these books by himself?" "What kinds of sources will satisfy this woman, and how long will she wait for an answer?" Sometimes it may help to ask them questions as well (such as, "Would you like me to come with you or can you find it on your own?").

Good reference librarians also evaluate their own performance. They check themselves as they work. As you're helping a patron, you may see logical inconsistencies in what you are finding and realize you need to approach things differently, correcting your spelling, for instance, or choosing different keywords to search with. Sometimes you may feel the need to verify your findings in another source, or to consult with a colleague about other possible sources of information. As your goal is always to provide the patrons with the best information possible to help answer their questions, you should never hesitate to share with them any qualms you might have about the reliability of information or to ask others for assistance.

Troubleshooting Technology

Finally, in today's hi-tech world, librarians often spend a lot of time troubleshooting technology to help their patrons. It is crucial to develop a basic understanding of the equipment in your library: the computers, the printers, the copy machines, and how to fix their little glitches. In the remaining chapters of this book, I will spend more time discussing communication, searching, and evaluation. I will *not* discuss how to deal with technology that does not always behave as expected. To offer your patrons excellent reference service, however, at a minimum it is necessary to know how to reboot a computer, reattach cables that have been pulled out, download and upload files, e-mail search results, and change the toner in printers and copy machines. Learn as much as you can about the computers, printers and other machines in your library, and build relationships with people you can call on when you encounter technological problems that are beyond your capabilities.

Access to new technologies and the Internet has transformed many small libraries, enabling them to offer more comprehensive access to information and services than ever before, enhancing their visibility, and attracting new patrons.[4] Librarians working in small communities are often masterful at identifying knowledgeable people they can call on in their moments of technological need in order to keep their equipment up and running. It is also essential to cultivate your own knowledge and understanding of technology and computer maintenance to best serve your community.

WHAT DOES IT MEAN TO PROVIDE EXCELLENT REFERENCE SERVICE?

How do you know when you are providing excellent service? You may choose from a variety of ways to evaluate reference service.[5] We have already touched on the need to evaluate the sources you use and to informally assess the needs of your patrons and your own abilities as you provide service. There are many more formal ways to evaluate reference service, including surveying your patrons and having people "test" you by posing questions.

In a small library, where you may have few resources and little time to conduct formal evaluations, you may need to take a more practical approach in figuring out how to provide first-rate reference service. One thing you can easily do is to educate yourself with regard to the resources available and the search techniques needed to use them. You can also draw on some of the research others have done on what makes library users feel welcome and willing to ask for assistance again. For instance, research has shown that patrons like being greeted immediately by a librarian as they approach him or her,[6] that they appreciate knowing the librarian's name,[7] and that they feel better able to communicate with librarians whom they perceive as being "genuine."[8] We know that patrons value enthusiasm, interest, and helpfulness on the part of librarians[9]; indeed, some patrons value the interpersonal aspects of interacting with librarians more than the information they may receive from them![10] And we know that when librarians are approachable and courteous, patrons are more likely to want to return to them for service.[11]

Much of the research on what makes for excellent reference service has been incorporated into the RUSA (Reference and Users Services Association) "Guidelines for Behavioral Performance,"[12] which are discussed further in Chapter 2. But it is clear that patrons value librarians who are approachable, interested in their questions, and willing to help.

IN SUM

If you work in a small community, you are "The Librarian." You may be the sole person (or the only full-time person) responsible for maintaining the library building; ordering, cataloging, and circulating books and other materials; managing meeting spaces; signing up volunteers; and of course, providing personal assistance to users and potential users of information, that is, providing reference service. People generally appreciate libraries and perceive them as "nice places" to be[13]; your personal touch, as well as your skills in finding and evaluating information, can help your library prosper and fulfill its role as a vibrant gathering place where people come for information, education, and entertainment.

REVIEW

1.   Can you briefly define reference service?
2.   What are the main activities involved in providing reference service?

3.   What skills and qualities do you already possess that you believe will help you provide excellent reference service to your patrons? What are some things you would like to improve?

NOTES

1.   Green, S. S. (1876). Personal relations between librarians and readers. *Library Journal, 1,* 74–81. Available online at http://polaris.gseis.ucla.edu/jrichardson/DIS220/personal.htm

2.   Reference and Adult Services Division. (1990). *Information services for information consumers: Guidelines for providers.* Chicago: RASD, American Library Association.

3.   For a more technical discussion, see RUSA's *Definitions of reference transactions,* Available online at http://www.ala.org/ala/rusa/protools/referenceguide/definitionsreference.cfm.

4.   Heuertz, L., Gordon, A. C., Gordon, M. T., Moore, E. J. (2003). The impact of public access computing on rural and small town libraries. *Rural Libraries, 23* (1), 51–79.

5.   Whitlatch, J. B. (2000). *Evaluating reference services: A practical guide.* Chicago: American Library Association.

6.   Gothberg, H. M. (1976). Immediacy: A study of communication effect on the reference process. *Journal of Academic Librarianship, 2,* 126–29.

7.   Durrance, J. C. (1995). Factors that influence reference success: What makes questioners willing to return? In J. B. Whitlatch (Ed.), *Library users and reference services* (pp. 243–265). Binghamton, NY: The Haworth Press.

8.   Crouch, R. K. (1982). Interpersonal communication in the reference interview. Ph.D. Thesis, University of Toronto (Canada). Abstract obtained from ProQuest Dissertations and Theses.

9.   Whitlatch, J. B. (1990). *The role of the academic reference librarian.* New York: Greenwood Press.

10.   Radford, M. L. (1999). *The reference encounter: Interpersonal communication in the academic library.* Chicago: Association of College and Research Libraries.

11.   Durrance, "Factors that influence reference success."

12.   Reference & User Services Association. Guidelines for Behavioral Performance of Reference and Information Service Providers. Available online at http://www.ala.org/ala/rusa/protools/referenceguide/guidelinesbehavioral.cfm

13.   Vavrek, B. (1990). *Assessing the information needs of rural Americans.* Clarion, PA: College of Library Science, Center for the Study of Rural Librarianship, Clarion University of Pennsylvania. pp. 18–19.

CHAPTER 2

Communicating with Your Patrons

The average "interview" is simply a matter of chatting, no matter how briefly, with another individual about his or her wants.[1]

Communication skills are at the heart of reference service. Having sound knowledge of basic types of information sources and how to search and evaluate them is important, of course, but having good communication and interpersonal skills is absolutely essential. In fact, a research study found that the *most important factor* contributing to good reference service was following recommended professional practices for interviewing library users.[2] In this chapter, we examine the reference process, particularly *the reference interview,* and review the behavioral guidelines for librarians recommended by ALA's Reference and User Services Association (RUSA). Along the way we'll encounter examples of questions and you can consider how you, as a librarian, might wish to respond to them.

THE INFORMATION NEEDS OF PATRONS

The reference process actually begins before the patron, or library user, ever makes contact with you. It is important to remember that the reference process is not so much about you, the librarian, as it is about your patrons and their information needs.

As we make our way through life, there are moments at which we hit stopping points, moments when we feel a *need* for further information that will allow us to make worthwhile decisions, or to proceed a little further toward our goals. When people describe these moments, they say things like, "I hit a wall"; "I came to a fork in the road"; "I lost my way."[3] In the language of librarianship, we would say these people have *information needs.*

People with information needs must take some kind of action to move forward. They may talk to friends, family, or acquaintances; they may consult their own collection of books, or log on to the Internet from home for a quick Google search. In some cases, they may come to you, the librarian, with their information need. Studies have shown that the library is generally *not* the first place people tend to go with their information needs.[4] This implies that perhaps the first part of "communication" involves marketing your library, making people aware of its existence and the services that you offer, and ensuring that the library is a warm and welcoming environment. Many people *do* think of the library when they have certain kinds of information needs, and you must stand ready to help them.

Once the person with the information need decides to approach you (the librarian), what happens next? For decades researchers have analyzed the interaction between patron and librarian, often known as *the reference interview.* They have debated about whether the reference interview is an art or a science[5] and have noted that, of course, every interview is different depending on the people involved and their needs, wishes, and constraints. Still, there is a general process to be aware of and some helpful techniques worth mastering.

THE REFERENCE INTERVIEW

A useful way to approach the reference interview is to break it into five parts:[6]

1. Open the interview.
2. Negotiate the question.
3. Search for information.
4. Communicate the information to the user.
5. Close the interview.

Open the Interview

In opening the reference interview, you will want to greet the patron, make him or her feel welcome, and offer your assistance. It is not enough to wait passively for a patron to find you; it is your job to reach out to the patron with a friendly greeting. One of the great benefits of working in a small library is that you are acquainted with many of the people who walk through the door and can greet them by name; they know you, too.

It is important to make each person who enters the library (or phones, or e-mails) feel welcome, even if you don't know them or are not really very fond of them; it is your professional responsibility to make the library's resources accessible to every member of the community. Welcoming greetings usually involve a smile and some variation of:

"Hi! How can I help you?" or
"How are you today? What can I help you with?"

Body language is an essential part of in-person reference service. Smiling, making eye contact with the patron, using a warm tone of voice, and having an open posture are all ways you can put your patrons at ease.[7] Be aware of your patron's facial expressions, posture, and tone of voice as well. Some questions may be difficult to articulate or embarrassing to ask; in such cases, patrons may appear uncomfortable, avoid looking directly at you, or use a very hushed voice as they pose a question. It is important to respect a patron's wish for a quiet conversation and to proceed gently (but professionally) when dealing with sensitive topics.

At the same time, it is vital for you to communicate your genuine interest in helping the patron with his or her question. This does not mean you have to be personally interested in every single question posed; you are interested in helping patrons with their information needs, and that is enough. Expressions of interest include affirmations ("uh-huh," "yes," "I see") as well as statements such as, "That sounds fascinating!" "What a great topic!"

Finally, listen carefully as your patron poses the initial question. You will want to listen throughout the reference interview, so you may as well get started! Don't hesitate to jot down notes as the patron is speaking, if you find that this helps you.

Negotiate the Question

After a patron has expressed an initial information need, you may find that you need to probe a bit more deeply to truly be of assistance. This involves asking the user appropriate questions about what it is he or she needs. Question negotiation is one of the most hotly debated aspects of reference work. Some librarians swear that library users rarely ask up-front for what they really need[8]; others believe that the idea of interviewing patrons is completely overrated.[9]

The truth is probably somewhere in between: while many questions are straightforward and will probably not require much probing, you will have people ask you questions that do not truly represent their underlying information needs.[10] In some cases, this may be because the patron is trying to present the question according to what he or she thinks the library will have available. For instance, someone interested in locating information about Saudi Arabia may ask, "Where are your encyclopedias?" because she remembers consulting an encyclopedia when she did a report on India back when she was in junior high school. In other cases, your patrons may still be figuring out what it is they actually need. For instance, a young man who asks, "Do you have any books on travel?" may be debating whether he wants to spend his hard-earned money visiting friends in New York City or backpacking on the Appalachian Trail. In either of these cases, asking a few questions can help patrons express more specifically what they are really after.

In other instances patrons are reluctant to share their "real" question because of modesty or embarrassment, or simply because they do not know you very well. A tearful teenager who asks for "the books on relationships" may respond to a few gentle clarifying questions as to what kinds of books might be helpful but probably won't want to elaborate too much on what's behind her request. At times like these, you must balance your desire to understand the real question with the need to respect the patron's privacy.

Bearing in mind the limits of question negotiation, what are some of the best ways to find out what the patron really wants? Here are some tried and true techniques.

Ask Open Questions to Get the Patron to Open Up

Open questions are those that elicit open-ended responses, thus allowing the patron to talk freely about what he or she might like. For instance:

Patron 1:   I need to get some articles for my English paper.
Librarian: Sure! What's your paper about?

Patron 2:   I'd like a little help tracking down some legal forms.
Librarian: Okay! What kind of forms are you looking for?

A particular subset of open questions known as *neutral questions* can be useful in getting patrons to talk a bit more about their underlying needs, the situation in which they arose, and how they plan to use the information without directly asking, "Why do you want this information?" (which may cause people to tense up). Here are a few examples of "neutral questions" you might ask:

"Could you tell me little bit about the problem you're working on?"
"What would you like to know about [topic]?"
"Tell me a bit about how you plan to use this information."[11]

Research has shown that the *very first question* the librarian asks matters, and librarians who begin their negotiation by asking an open question are more likely to discover what the patron actually needs.[12] This doesn't mean, however, that open questions are always needed, or that they are the only kinds of questions worth asking.

Ask Closed Questions if You Need the Patron to Focus

Closed questions are those that elicit a yes/no or this/that response. For example:

Patron 3:   I'd like to read a book about President George W. Bush.

Librarian: It looks like the only book we have here in the library was written in the year 2000, before he was elected president; is that alright?

Patron 4:   My teacher asked us to summarize one article from this week's issue of *Time* magazine for our current events class.

Librarian: Would you like to look at the magazine online, or would you prefer to look at the print version?

This kind of question can be useful when the patron's need seems fairly clear to you, but there are some straightforward choices to be made with regard to the information available.

Summarize the Question, as You Understand It, to the Patron

Rephrasing can be useful for making sure that you have a solid understanding of the question; it invites the patron to correct your understanding or expound on their needs a bit further before you get into searching for information.

Here is a sample opening and negotiation, using open and closed questions and a summary:

Librarian: Hi, how may I help you?

Patron 5:   I need some information on Marie Curie.

Librarian: Alright! What would you like to know about Marie Curie?

Patron 5:   [looking at what appears to be an assignment sheet]: Um, I need to find out about her family life, her education, and especially her scientific discoveries.

Librarian: Okay, I'm sure we can find some information on those things! Is this for a school assignment?

Patron 5:   Yeah, it's for my biology paper.

Librarian: Oh, for biology! What grade are you in?

Patron 5:   Ninth.

Librarian: Did your teacher say anything about the types of sources you're supposed to use?

Patron 5:   [looking at sheet again]: Um, she said we had to have at least two journal articles and a book, and that it was okay to use Internet sources, too.

Librarian: Great! So just to make sure I understand: you need some information about Marie Curie's family life, education, and scientific discoveries for your biology paper, and it's okay to use Internet sources but you also need at least two articles and a book.

Patron 5:   That's right.
Librarian: Okay! Let's see what we can find.

Note how the librarian maintains a friendly, interested tone. She asks the patron to tell her about the question in broad terms and follows up on the clues she sees (i.e., the assignment sheet the patron is holding) to get a sense of the type of material that might be appropriate. Then she summarizes the question to make sure she has everything right. Now the two of them are ready to search for information.

Search for Information

Once you have a good sense of the patron's needs, you can begin to search for information. Much of this book is devoted to discussing particular sources and approaches to searching them; however, here are a few general rules to bear in mind:

- Before you dive in, take a moment to think clearly about what types of sources would be appropriate to answer this person's question. If this person wants books, you will immediately think, "Library catalog!" If articles seem appropriate for answering questions, consider what databases you have access to and the level of writing that they will want or need.

- If possible, include the patron in your search. Chances are good that the user knows more about the topic and about what will and won't work than you do even if you are a terrific "reference interviewer." This means that the patron can help brainstorm search terms and strategies and, working with you, can move the search in useful directions. One of the most useful aspects of searching alongside the patron is that he or she can provide you with immediate feedback as to whether what you are finding may be helpful. If you're working at a computer, make sure the patron can see the screen and know what you are doing; likewise, if you're consulting a print source, show the patron the book and how you are searching it.

  Including the patron as you search may be more difficult if you are talking with someone over the phone or e-mailing him or her. You can still describe your search strategy to the "remote" patron, however, so that he or she can be fully aware of what you did and suggest further action as needed (or continue the search himself or herself).

- Evaluate as you search. Remember that you will constantly be evaluating sources (in terms of accuracy, authority, content, currency, and organization) and the patron's satisfaction with them. You will need to check your search strategy as well. If you don't seem to be coming up with the information you think is available, you may need to rethink your search terms or reconsider the sources you are searching.

Communicate the Information to the User

If the library patron is standing at your elbow, it is quite possible that you are communicating "answers" to him or her as you search. Even so, it is useful to consider how you can best package the information so that the patron walks away with useful information in a format he or she can easily use. This may mean you do some of the following:

- Print out or write down things for your patrons, such as titles and call numbers of books, names of databases, phone numbers and contact information, search strategies that they can try again on their own, article citations, the full text of articles.

- Make sure that patrons understand what you are saying. For instance, if you start talking about *citations* and a patron gives you a blank look, perhaps he or she doesn't know what the term *citation* means and you should rephrase it: "Here are some titles of articles and the magazines in which they appear." If there are further steps needed to retrieve books or articles, verify that patrons are comfortable taking these steps on their own. Remain open to new questions or ideas patrons may have.

- Make clear to the patron the *process* you are going through to find the information. One of the goals of libraries is to make people more self-sufficient in their search for information, and modeling the process of information seeking is one way of doing this. If a patron is at your side, you might narrate as you go along. For example:

Patron 6:   I need some information on how many abortions there are in the United States each year.

Librarian: Okay, let's see what we can find. For statistics, the first place I like to look is the *Statistical Abstract of the U.S.,* which is a book of statistics that the government puts out each year. I keep it handy, right here by the desk. You're interested in how many people have abortions in the United States each year, so let's check the index for "abortion." Okay, see here? This says we'll find some information in Tables 93, 94, and 95. Let's see, there we go! It looks like in the year 2002, 1,293,000 abortions were performed in the United States.

Or you might coach patrons through their searches in the catalog or database, letting them type but guiding them through the process and explaining what they are seeing as they move along.

- Avoid overwhelming patrons with information. Sometimes librarians feel a compulsion to find every possible bit of information they think will be useful to the inquirer, but bear in mind that we work with information all day and probably have a higher threshold for "information overload" than many of our patrons. If patrons are thanking you repeatedly, their eyes are glazing over, and they're starting to back away, chances are, you've given them enough information, at least for now!

- *Always* cite the source of your information: this is the trademark of a librarian! Try to explain to patrons why the information you are providing is authoritative or what biases you believe a source might have. For example:

Patron 7:   How do you pronounce this word? [Points to the word "obfuscate"].

Librarian: Let's look that up in the Merriam-Webster online dictionary to see how it's pronounced. They've been putting out dictionaries for many years, and they have a nice feature that lets us hear the word!

Or, if you are uncertain a source provides "the full picture," you might say something like this: "It looks like you've found some interesting information on the Chevron Web site discussing why gas prices are so high, but it's important to remember that this is from the perspective of a major oil company. I think you'll want to balance this out with some additional magazine or newspaper articles."

Close the Interview

When it seems the patron has enough information to work with, the time has come to close the interview. Oftentimes, your patrons will close the interview by thanking you, thus indicating satisfaction with the information received. A great response is: "You're welcome, and please feel free to come back if you have any more questions." If the patron doesn't make the first move (and you believe the question has been answered), you can ask something like, "Does that look good to you?" or "Do you feel like that's enough to get you started?"

No matter who makes the first move to close the interview, many librarians like to verify that patrons are satisfied with the information they have received. Asking simple questions such as "Does that help? Is there anything else I can help you with?" or "Does that answer your question?" can give you a sense of whether the library user is satisfied. It's always a good idea to end the reference interview with a statement encouraging patrons to feel free to return to you, should any additional questions arise.

In fact, just as the reference process begins before a patron ever says a word, it may continue after an interview is officially "closed." As patrons consider the information you have helped them locate, they may find they have further questions and may return to you for additional guidance (or with a completely new idea to pursue). When a patron returns, take it as a sign that you have succeeded in gaining his or her trust and have left the door open for the patron to ask for assistance. If the patron lingers in the library consulting books or other sources, check back to see how the work is going.

RUSA GUIDELINES FOR BEHAVIORAL PERFORMANCE

A useful set of guidelines for librarians to follow when conducting reference interviews is put out by the Reference and User Services Association (RUSA) of the American Library Association, and is available online at http://www.ala.org/ala/rusa/ protools/referenceguide/guidelinesbehavioral.cfm. These guidelines are a useful reminder of the behaviors exemplified by the best reference librarians. According to RUSA, these behaviors are:

1. Approachability: In order to have a successful reference transaction, patrons must be able to identify that a reference librarian is available to provide assistance and also must feel comfortable in going to that person for help. In remote environments, this also means placing contact information for chat, email, telephone, and other services in prominent locations, to make them obvious and welcoming to patrons. Approachability behaviors, such as the initial verbal and non-verbal responses of the librarian, will set the tone for the entire communication process, and will influence the depth and level of interaction between the staff and the patrons. At this stage in the process, the behaviors exhibited by the staff member should serve to welcome the patrons and to place them at ease. The librarian's role in the communications process is to make the patrons feel comfortable in a situation that may be perceived as intimidating, risky, confusing, and overwhelming.

2. Interest: A successful librarian must demonstrate a high degree of interest in the reference transaction. While not every query will contain stimulating intellectual challenges, the librarian should be interested in each patron's informational need and should be committed to providing the most effective assistance. Librarians who demonstrate a high level of interest in the inquiries of their patrons will generate a higher level of satisfaction among users.

3. Listening/Inquiring: The reference interview is the heart of the reference transaction and is crucial to the success of the process. The librarian must be effective in identifying the patron's information needs and must do so in a manner that keeps patrons at ease. Strong listening and questioning skills are necessary for a positive interaction.

4. Searching: The search process is the portion of the transaction in which behavior and accuracy intersect. Without an effective search, not only is the desired information unlikely to be found, but patrons may become discouraged as well. Yet many of the aspects of searching that lead to accurate results are still dependent on the behavior of the librarian.

5. Follow-up: The reference transaction does not end when the librarian leaves the patrons. The librarian is responsible for determining if the patrons are satisfied with the results of the search, and is also responsible for referring the patrons to other sources, even when those sources are not available in the local library.[13]

Effective techniques for conveying approachability and interest, and for listening/inquiring, searching, and following up with patrons are listed under each of the five behaviors. Because librarians often receive questions over the phone or via e-mail or chat, RUSA also provides suggestions for communicating with these "remote" patrons. Take a moment to review the full set of Guidelines online. It's well worth your time.

WHAT IF YOU CAN'T ANSWER?

All of these "reference interview" suggestions may sound just great, but, especially if you are new to library work, a question may be nagging at you: What if I can't answer the patron's question? Here are a few comforting thoughts:

- Nobody can answer every question correctly. Several studies have shown that when confronted with "typical" preselected ready reference questions, librarians give accurate responses only about 55 percent of the time.[14] Studies including other types of questions have shown higher rates of librarian success,[15] but the point is, there will be some tough questions that you cannot answer.

- Do your best—and then refer. When you encounter a difficult question, stretch your interpersonal and search skills to their limits. Listen closely to what the patron is saying; ask as many clarifying questions as you need to; think carefully about the best sources and search strategies; and don't be afraid to keep trying variations on your search. One thing that sets the professionals apart from the amateurs is the willingness to persist in a search, to reiterate the search using different sources or different search terms.

If you still aren't coming up with a workable answer, consider referring the patron to another organization you think might hold the answer, or to a larger library. Or if the patron has time, offer to continue searching (or consult with colleagues) and to e-mail or phone the patron later on.

- It gets easier with practice. One of the rewarding aspects of reference work is that as you come to know and understand your patrons, hear certain questions for a second or third time, and master different types of sources and search techniques, your job *will* become easier. At the same time, there is generally enough variety in reference work—new patrons, new questions, new sources—to keep things interesting. Although your initial learning curve may be steep, and you may feel a bit overwhelmed at first, hang in there!

- People will appreciate your trying. Even if you can't find the perfect answer every time, generally speaking, your patrons will be grateful for your sincere efforts on their behalf. Bear in mind that many people value the interpersonal aspects of reference as much as, or more than, the information they receive.

WHAT IF THE PATRON BECOMES ANGRY?

Your helpful attitude is an excellent safeguard against angry patrons; however, every community has its share of irate individuals. People may be frustrated with their own inability to find an answer, with the circumstances surrounding the question (a broken home appliance, a misbehaving child, a report for a hated class), or with other aspects of their lives over which you have no control. Patience and professionalism go a long way in the face of hostility: Try to maintain your aura of approachability and willingness to help, overlook rude comments or rolling eyes, and present information tactfully.

If someone demands to speak with a "higher authority," calmly provide them with contact information for your supervisor or board of trustees, and write down everything that happened as soon as possible, while it is still fresh in your memory. And should a patron become truly hostile or threatening, have ready a plan of action for summoning help from the police and/or people nearby, particularly if you are running a one-person library. Libraries are generally peaceful places, but it is best to be prepared.

IN SUM

Welcoming your patrons to the library, gaining an understanding of their information needs, and helping them resolve those needs is the essence of reference work. Communication skills go hand in hand with effective searching skills; master both and you will be an exceptional librarian!

REVIEW

1. What are the five parts of the reference interview?
2. What are three ways to demonstrate *approachability* and *interest* to your patrons?
3. What are *open, closed,* and *neutral* questions? Give an example of each. When might these types of questions come in handy during the reference interview?
4. How might you respond to these patrons with an open question?

   [from a young girl]: Could you help me find a book on cats?
   [from a senior citizen]: I'm looking for some information on diabetes.
   [from a teenager]: Where are your CDs?
   [from a mother with two small children]: Do you have something that would help me stay sane?

5.   Why is it important to cite your source to the patron?

6.   What is meant by *follow-up,* and why does it matter?

7.   How might you respond to the following question:

> *[from a distressed looking man]:* I've been looking for half an hour for something that would help my son do better in school, and you just don't seem to have anything! I only saw some stuff from like, the 1960s or something. Don't you ever get any new books around here?

NOTES

1.   Katz, W.A. (2002). *Introduction to reference work* (8th ed.). Boston: McGraw-Hill, p. 124.

2.   Saxton, M.L., & Richardson, J.V. (2002). *Understanding reference transactions: Transforming an art into a science.* San Diego, CA: Academic Press, p. 99.

3.   Dervin, B. (1977). Useful theory for librarianship: Communication not information. *Drexel Library Quarterly, 13,* 16–32.

4.   Katz, W.A. (2002). *Introduction to reference work,* vol. 2: *Reference services and reference processes* (8th ed.), Chapter 2. New York: McGraw Hill.

5.   Saxton & Richardson, *Understanding reference transactions.*

6.   Taken directly from Richard Bopp, 2001, p. 48. In Bopp, R.E., & Smith, L.C. (2001). *Reference and information services: An introduction* (3rd ed.). Englewood, CO: Libraries Unlimited.

7.   Harris, R.M. & Michell, G. (1986). The social context of reference work: Assessing the effects of gender and communication skill on observers' judgments of competence. *Library and Information Science Research, 8,* 85–101; Michell, G., & Harris, R.M. (1987). Evaluating the reference interview: Some factors influencing patrons and professionals. *RQ, 27*(1), 95–105.

8.   Mount, E. (1966). Communication barriers and the reference question. *Special Libraries, 57*(8), 575–78.

9.   Sarah Weissman, qtd in Janes, J. (2003). *Introduction to reference work in the digital age.* New York: Neal-Schuman, p. 53.

10.   Lynch, M.J. (1977). Reference interviews in public libraries. *Library Quarterly, 48* (2), 119–42; Ford, C.E. *An exploratory study of the differences between face-to-face and computer-mediated reference interactions.* Ph.D. Thesis, Indiana University, 2003.

11.   Dervin, B., & Dewdney, P. (1986). Neutral questioning: A new approach to the reference interview. *RQ, 25*(4), 506–13.

12.   Durrance, J.C. (1995). Factors that influence reference success: What makes questioners willing to return? In J.B. Whitlach (Ed.), *Library users and reference services* (pp. 243–65). Binghamton, NY: The Haworth Press.

13.   Excerpted from Reference & User Services Association. Guidelines for Behavioral Performance of Reference and Information Service Providers. Available at http://www.ala.org/ala/rusa/protools/referenceguide/guidelinesbehavioral.cfm

14.   Hernon, P. & McClure, C. (1986, April 15). Unobtrusive reference testing: The 55% rule. *Library Journal, 111,* 37–41.

15.   Saxton & Richardson, *Understanding reference transactions.*

CHAPTER 3

Building and Maintaining a Reference Collection

Libraries have expanded the traditional view and definition of collections so that the concept no longer equates with those materials that the library "owns."[1]

In addition to your excellent communication skills, it is of course essential to have at hand some resources for you and your patrons to draw on in your quest for information. And wow, what choices we have! Today's libraries offer their users a cornucopia of information sources. This holds true for even the smallest library with an Internet connection. Printed books, online databases, and a multitude of freely available Web pages are just waiting to be used. So, how do you go about identifying those sources that will be helpful to your patrons?

This chapter provides an overview of the types of sources considered to be "reference" sources and provides some quick guidelines for selecting, evaluating, and maintaining a collection of these sources. Chapters 5 through 9 discuss specific types of sources (and titles) and their appropriate uses.

WHAT KINDS OF SOURCES MAKE UP A REFERENCE COLLECTION?

Back in the old days, the reference section of the library held a distinct collection of books that people could "refer" to for bits of information but generally didn't want to read all the way through from cover to cover. Some of these books, such as bibliographies, indexes, and abstracts, organized and provided access to other sources. Others, such as encyclopedias, dictionaries, biographical sources, atlases, and "ready reference" (or fact) sources, contained specific types of information that might be of interest to library patrons.[2]

How times have changed! Reference collections today are a mixture of books and electronic sources of various sorts: the library catalog, resources that are freely available on the Web, databases purchased by individual libraries or through consortia, specific titles on CD-ROM or DVD.[3] The growth of electronic resources means that your "collection" is not limited to what is held in the library; you and your patrons have access to resources that are housed and hosted elsewhere. It also means that patrons may not have to visit the library to take advantage of library resources; they may tap into your Web pages, your catalog, and some of your databases from outside the library building. And of course, this has implications for providing service to these "remote" users.

Although the reference environment may have grown more complicated, some things have remained constant. While they may now be available electronically, many of the *types* of sources that we have traditionally thought of as "reference" sources are still around, helping librarians provide information to patrons. These include library catalogs and bibliographies that you can use to locate books; indexes that provide access to articles in newspapers, magazines and journals (and now, often include the full text of the articles); encyclopedias, dictionaries, biographical and geographical sources; and "ready reference" (factual) sources.[4] To be sure, there are some new types of resources to consider as well, such as Internet search engines, mapping software, and "aggregated" databases that bring together all kinds of information in a subject area. This is no cause for alarm; you don't have to know everything about every kind of reference source that's out there by tomorrow! You do, however, owe it to your patrons to be open to exploring new resources and new technologies.

DEVELOPING AND MANAGING A REFERENCE COLLECTION

In selecting materials for your reference collection, there are some general **collection development guidelines** to bear in mind. You probably already have a collection development policy for your library collection as a whole. The reference collection is a bit different, in that you are not focusing here on books or audiovisual materials that the public will be checking out and taking home; however, many of the basic principles of collection development still apply.

Know Your Community

To select wisely, you must first consider the needs of the people in your community, along with the mission and goals of the library.[5] A clear understanding of the history of your community, its major businesses and other organizations, and the social and economic status of the people in the area your library serves is vitally important in developing all library collections including the reference collection.

Census data, such as that found at American FactFinder (http://factfinder.census.gov), is extremely useful for showing, in general terms, things such as the distribution of ages and genders, the ethnic and racial composition, the educational level, and the economic standing of people in your community. If census data show that there are a large number of older adults in your community, for instance, you may want to be sure the reference collection includes resources on health issues; if there are many native Spanish speakers, you may want to consider relevant Spanish-language titles. Besides reviewing census data, other useful strategies for understanding what types of resources are needed include talking with long-time members of the community, holding a community forum to find out what people would like the library to provide, or even conducting a more formal survey of library patrons.[6]

In addition to being aware of the general needs of your patrons (and potential patrons), keep an eye out for specialized resources pertaining to your geographical region. For example, small libraries in Kentucky may wish to acquire the *Kentucky Encyclopedia,* whereas those in Minnesota probably will not.

Make Use of Standard Selection Aids

A number of well-known selection aids are available to help you develop your reference collection. Some are very comprehensive such as the American Library Association's *Guide to Reference* (12th edition forthcoming) or *American Reference Books Annual* (available online as *ARBAOnline*), which includes thousands of reviews of reference sources each year. Others, such as the following, are geared toward helping smaller libraries:

O'Gorman, Jack (Ed.). *Reference sources for small and medium-sized libraries* (7th ed.). Chicago: American Library Association, 2007.

Sweetland, James H. *Fundamental reference sources.* Chicago: American Library Association, 2001.

Lewis, Audrey. *Madame Audrey's guide to mostly cheap but good reference books for small and rural libraries.* Chicago: American Library Association, 1998.

Graff Hysell, Shannon. *Recommended reference books for small and medium-sized libraries and media centers.* Westport, CT: Libraries Unlimited (a subset of books appearing in ARBA, compiled annually).

Each of these texts includes categorized lists of potentially useful reference material. It's not a bad idea to familiarize yourself with a couple of these books. Even if many of the sources listed in them appear irrelevant to your library or outdated, they can give you ideas of the types of resources that are available, and you can always check for an up-to-date version.

In addition to these book-length compilations of recommended reference books, also keep an eye on the reference books reviewed in the sources you consult as you build your general library collection. You probably rely on magazines such as *Booklist, American Libraries, Library Journal,* or other reviewing sources to build your collection. Each of these publications includes reviews of reference sources as well; *American Libraries* and *Library Journal* have special issues covering "best reference sources" (the May and April 15 issues, respectively). And of course, Amazon.com and the major vendors (such as Baker & Taylor or Ingram) can be used to pull up editorial reviews of these sources.

Some states or regional consortia provide their public libraries with current recommendations for core reference collections. For example, the Standards Committee of the Alabama Library Association provides "Suggestions for a Basic Reference Collection" for the state's public libraries at http://www.apls.state.al.us/webpages/pubs/standards basicrefcoll.pdf. Check to see if your state library or consortium maintains such a list.

Freely available Web resources are a very important component of today's reference collection. You will probably want to put together one or more Web pages that your patrons can quickly access for reference sources. Useful reference portals, which provide categorized links to numerous freely available reference sources, include the Internet Public Library's (IPL) reference section (http://www.ipl.org/div/subject/browse/ref00.00.00), the Librarians' Internet Index (http://lii.org/pub/topic/reference), Library Spot (http://www.libraryspot.com), and Refdesk.com (http://www.refdesk.com/facts.html). These kinds of resources are discussed in more detail in Chapter 9. Looking at these sites can give you some great ideas for ways to categorize your own collection of online reference links, as well as an appreciation of the amount of material that's freely available online. For instance, the IPL includes resources in the following categories: *Almanacs, Associations & Organizations, Biographies, Calculation & Conversion Tools, Calendars, Census Data & Demographics, Dictionaries, Encyclopedias, Experts & How-To, Genealogy, Geography, Grammars, News & Current Events, Periodical Directories, Quotations, Style and Writing Guides, Telephone and Address, Time & Weather,* and *Trivia.* Which of these categories and their underlying resources might merit inclusion in your online reference collection?

Many state libraries also offer links to valuable online sources that you can link to or select from as you build your collection. For instance, as a part of the Kansas State Library's "Blue Skyways" service, librarians have compiled lists of useful Internet sources, including "Kansas Information" (see http://skyways.lib.ks.us/library/refe rence). Another example is the Indiana State Library's "ISL Quick Guide" (http:// www.statelib.lib.in.us/www/quikguide.html), which links to a number of free general reference sources and many Indiana-specific Web resources as well. Your state library may provide similar pages of reference sources from which to pick and choose.

Strive for Balance

Your library's collections are meant to respond to the needs of all members of the community[7]; and the reference collection is no exception. Be sure to allocate funds specifically for reference materials, as well as for circulating material. Anne Gervasi and Betty Kay Seibt suggest that you should also "always have a list of needed reference materials at hand to suggest to the patron who wants to make a donation."[8] In addition to practical titles, there are some beautiful reference sources—historical atlases, pictorial histories, and birdwatchers' field guides—that many patrons would be proud to donate to the library.

As you develop the reference collection, consider the needs of different segments of the population in your community: the young as well as the old, people with different educational backgrounds, and from different races and ethnicities. You'll also be striving to maintain a balance between the educational and entertainment missions of the library: Should you replace that well-worn version of the *Guinness Book of World Records* or spring for a new *Merck Manual of Diagnosis and Therapy*? And you'll find yourself trying to strike a balance between print and electronic resources. Which works better for your patrons? Which is more affordable? Watch how your patrons use the collection, analyze the questions you receive, and keep your mind as open as you possibly can when it comes to new types of library users, new questions, and new technologies.

Build on What's Already in Place

As you develop the reference collection in your small library, remember: you are not alone, laboring in isolation. You are part of a community of librarians. As a member of this community, you are building on the work of those who may have worked in your library before you, and can also rely on resources made available by other librarians and information specialists in your region, state, or throughout the world. Ask yourself:

- What do I already have in the reference collection?

   Every collection has its strengths and weaknesses. As you work with your patrons using the collection, you will become intimately aware of what's in good shape and where the gaps are. Remember to "count your blessings" as you work to fill the gaps in the collection.

- What reference materials are available through my state library or consortia?

    In addition to providing lists of print and online reference materials, many state libraries or consortia of public and academic libraries strive to support their citizens by providing statewide access to databases for library cardholders. Examples include South Carolina's Virtual Library, DISCUS (http://scdiscus.org), Wyoming's Go WYLD! (http://gowyld.net/dbases.html), and MeL, the Michigan e-Library (http://mel.org). What does your state or regional consortium provide? Make sure you're aware of the latest offerings available.

- What's out there for free?

    It's worth mentioning once more: those lists of freely available reference sources at places such as the Internet Public Library and Refdesk.com are there for you and your patrons. Take some time to work through some of these lists and consider which resources might be most appropriate for your patrons.

Maintain Your Collection

Maintaining a collection includes weeding the collection periodically, as well as repairing and replacing sources as needed.[9] In some ways this is similar to what you will do for the rest of your library collection. Reference collections, however, are usually weeded more frequently than the general collection.[10] Most libraries also maintain standing orders or regular schedules for purchasing certain reference titles. For instance, you may get a new edition of *Chase's Calendar of Events* or the *Physician's Desk Reference* every year and discard the old editions as new ones come in. You will probably want to have a rotating schedule (as your budget allows) for purchasing new editions of encyclopedias, travel guides, and other types of sources.

You'll want to maintain your reference Web pages as well, weeding old links that no longer work and updating the addresses for those that have changed. Fortunately, there are many tools to help keep your pages free of broken links. If your library uses Web design software such as Dreamweaver, you may have a link-checking solution at hand. Otherwise, you can try a free application such as REL Link Checker Lite (http://www.relsoftware.com/rlc/), Xenu's Link Sleuth (http://home.snafu.de/tilman/xenulink.html), or OCLC's Link Evaluator plug-in for the Mozilla Firefox browser (http://openly.oclc.org/linkevaluator/). Or, if you have only a page or two to check, it might be simpler to use a free online service such as the one provided by the World Wide Web Consortium at http://validator.w3.org/checklink.

Collection maintenance also involves keeping resources current. A few timely tips:

- Read the review sources mentioned earlier on a regular basis to look for relevant new titles
- Subscribe to "current awareness" services, to keep up-to-date with Web resources—for instance, the Internet Scout Project (http://scout.wisc.edu)

or the Librarian's Internet Index "New This Week" (http://www.lii.org/pub/htdocs/subscribe.htm).

- Subscribe to state or national library listservs, such as LIBREF-L (http://www.library.kent.edu/page/10391) or PUBLIB (http://lists.webjunction.org/publib).
- Listen to patron suggestions and requests for sources: What would they like to see in the reference collection?

EVALUATING REFERENCE SOURCES

In considering individual sources, or reviews of them, you will want to evaluate them according to **standard evaluation criteria** before adding them to your collection. Lists of criteria abound,[11] but they almost always take into account the following elements:

- Content
  What is this source about, exactly? Carefully read any reviews; if the source (or a preview) is available, examine the table of contents and/or any introductory matter explaining its scope and purpose. Is the content of this resource relevant for your patrons? In other words, will this resource be used? How does it fit in with the other sources in your collection? Is it unique, or does it duplicate other available resources?
- Audience
  Who is the source addressed to: scholars, the general public, children? Would some of your patrons fit into that audience?
- Authority
  Who is behind this source? Who are the publisher, the author(s), the editor(s)? What are their credentials? Check the information available in book or Web site reviews, and/or the information given in the reference source itself.
- Accuracy and completeness
  If the resource is available to you, look up a few things you know something about. For instance I have a strong interest in (and some knowledge of) Colombia and its history, and often find myself looking into encyclopedia entries on Colombian topics, checking biographical information on Colombian figures, or looking up Colombian towns and cities in geographical or travel sources as I assess new sources. This gives me a sense of the thoroughness of coverage and the accuracy of information. Do the same with a topic you're passionate about.
- Currency
  How old is this source? Book publication dates are easy enough to check; with Web sites, you may find yourself digging a bit to locate a "last updated" date. You may have to rely on your own sleuthing abilities: Does the information

provided seem current? Do links work? Remember, too, that age matters more with some topics than with others. The age of a Bible concordance probably isn't as important as the age of a medical encyclopedia!

- Organization

  Is the source well organized? Organization is key to reference work. When looking at a book, consider the layout, the use of fonts, the clarity of the table of contents, the presence of a good index, and the use of cross references. When dealing with online sources, think about how readily the site lends itself to locating discrete bits of information: Is the layout clean and user-friendly? Is the site easily searchable? Do pages load quickly? Do ads or pop-ups distract you from finding information?

- Format

  With many sources now available in both print and electronic form, you may find yourself in a position of choosing one over the other. Each offers advantages. Electronic sources are highly searchable, easily manipulated, quickly updated, and, in many cases, available from both inside and outside the library. Print sources are highly reliable: they won't "crash," and the information you found in a book yesterday will still be there today, in the same location. And once you've paid for a book, it's yours: you'll still have access to it next year, and the year after that—assuming no one steals, loses, or damages it, that is! Which is better? The answer depends on what you plan to use a source for, how much issues like updating and remote access matter, how comfortable your patrons feel working with different types of formats—and, of course, price.

- Price

  In a perfect world, we would have limitless amounts of money to spend on our reference collections (both print and electronic) and price would not be a problem. Sadly, we do not live in such a world. As you evaluate sources, consider both the initial cost and whether it will be a recurring cost that your library can (and wishes to) absorb, as is the case with annual subscriptions to indexes and abstracts, as well as standing orders of various types. If you're truly operating on a shoestring, do your best to identify as many high-quality, freely available sources as possible for your patrons.

IN SUM

Your reference collection provides a vital cornerstone for service to your community. Building and maintaining it is a tall order, especially as it can encompass seemingly endless Web-based resources. But by paying attention to local needs, availing yourself of selection aids, and periodically taking stock of your strengths and weaknesses, you can make it a useful, responsive part of your library's collections.

REVIEW

1. What are some strategies you might use to determine which communities your library should be serving?
2. What are the main criteria by which you should evaluate reference sources?
3. What are three areas in which your library's reference collection needs more material? Can you identify an area that you feel is nicely developed?
4. Name three tools that will help you find out about new reference sources as they appear.
5. What kinds of reference sources (e.g., databases) does your state library offer to public library cardholders?

NOTES

1. Association of Research Libraries, Collections & Access Issues Task Force (2002). Collections & access for the 21st century scholar: Changing roles of research libraries. *ARL Bimonthly Report, 225.* Available online at http://www.arl.org/resources/pubs/br/br225/index.shtml
2. Katz, W.A. (1982). *Introduction to reference work* (4th ed.). Boston: McGraw-Hill.
3. Tenopir, C., & Ennis, L. (2002). A decade of digital reference: 1991–2001. *Reference & User Services Quarterly, 41*, 264–73.
4. See categories in Cassell, K.A., & Hiremath, U. (2006). *Reference and information services in the 21st century: An introduction.* New York: Neal-Schuman Publishers.
5. Johnson, P. (2004). *Fundamentals of collection development & management.* Chicago: American Library Association, p. 104.
6. Evans, G.E., & Saponaro, M.Z. (2000). *Developing library and information center collections* (4th ed.). Englewood, CO: Libraries Unlimited.
7. American Library Association. Library Bill of Rights (1996). Available online at http://www.ala.org/ala/oif/statementspols/statementsif/librarybillrights.htm
8. Gervasi, A., & Seibt, B.K. (1988). *Handbook for small, rural, and emerging public libraries.* Phoenix: Oryx Press, p. 116.
9. Johnson, *Fundamentals.*
10. ibid., p. 145.
11. For instance: *Critical evaluation of resources* (2007). Available online at the University of California, Berkeley Teaching Library Web site: http://www.lib.berkeley.edu/TeachingLib/Guides/Evaluation.html; *Critically analyzing information sources.* (2004). Available online at the Cornell University Library Web site: http://www.library.cornell.edu/olinuris/ref/research/skill26.htm; Beck, S.E. *The good, the bad & the ugly: Or, why it's a good idea to evaluate web sources.* (1997). Available online at the New Mexico State University Library Web site: http://lib.nmsu.edu/instruction/eval.html

CHAPTER 4

Searching Print and Electronic Sources

Knowledge is of two kinds. We know a subject ourselves, or we know where we can find information upon it.[1]

In addition to knowing *where* to find information on a particular subject, it is also important to know *how* to find information. Chapters 5 through 9 discuss some of the major types of reference sources available to help us understand where to find information. But before we begin to look at specific types of sources, it is useful to consider how we wish to approach these sources. This chapter quickly reviews some of the major techniques for finding information in print reference sources, in electronic databases, and on the Web.

SEARCHING IN PRINT REFERENCE SOURCES

Printed sources have evolved over the centuries to take on a certain uniformity, which makes them familiar to us and easy to handle in many ways. For instance, we can generally count on finding a title and an author (or editor) listed on the cover of a book and again on the spine. When we open that book, we can reasonably expect to find a title page with fuller information.

Several features of the average printed book provide us with organizational support:

- A table of contents outlines the major sections of the book and where they begin.
- A preface gives us a sense of what the book is about.
- Chapters or parts divide up the text in a logical order.
- An index or sometimes multiple indexes offer an alphabetical listing of topics, people, and/or titles mentioned in the book.
- Sequentially numbered pages allow us to make use of the information given in the table of contents and index, keying us into the location of material in the text.

Reference books generally share these useful features. Sometimes one or another of these characteristics will be exaggerated, and additional organizational aids will be present. For example, in the case of dictionaries, the text is divided up by thousands of **alphabetical entries** of words, instead of by just a few chapters, and guide words are often added at the top of each page to help us navigate. In the case of printed indexes, the **index** aspect expands to take over the entire book.

In navigating reference books, you will have frequent need to call on those two indispensable tools you mastered in kindergarten: numbers and the alphabet. In your first encounter with a new reference source, it's a good idea to read that title; check out the table of contents; skim the preface or introduction; and look through it, assessing not only the content, but also the arrangement: Is it alphabetical? Chronological? Hierarchical? Arranged by subject or theme? Are the entries numbered? What kinds of indexes does it contain?

The following sections outline the major organizational schemes of printed reference works.

Bibliographies

Organization varies greatly by purpose, scope, and topic. Shorter bibliographies may consist of a simple alphabetical listing of sources (by author or title). Longer bibliographies generally have more complex arrangements, by subject, date of publication, or format, for instance, often with room for different sorts of subdivisions within the broader categories. In these more complex bibliographies, additional indexes (author, title, and/or subject) are invariably included at the end of the work and help refer readers to specific page numbers and/or entry numbers.

Indexes and Abstracts

The most common arrangement found in printed indexes is to organize entries alphabetically by subject. Author indexes (and sometimes title indexes) may also be included. In some indexes and abstracts (for instance, in the print version of *Psychological Abstracts*), however, entries are grouped under subjects that are *not* arranged alphabetically, but rather according to a different kind of classification scheme. This type of arrangement generally requires users to consult a subject (or author) index, then turn to the appropriate page or entry number to find relevant information.

Encyclopedias

Alphabetical arrangement by subject is the norm for encyclopedias, although some are subdivided in interesting ways. Many print encyclopedias have traditionally offered supplementary yearbooks, several include chronologies of various types, and *Encyclopaedia Britannica's Propaeida* volume presents readers with a hierarchical outline of knowledge (the *Micropaedia* and *Macropaedia,* which form the bulk of the encyclopedia, are alphabetical by subject). Multivolume encyclopedias always include an extensive subject index, which offers cross references and helps readers find information that may be tucked away within broader articles. It's always a good idea to consult this index, even if you find a solid entry on your topic listed alphabetically in the encyclopedia, just to make sure you're not missing something good!

Dictionaries

Dictionaries, as we all know, are usually arranged alphabetically by entry word. Their cousins, the thesauri, may have straightforward alphabetical arrangements or may be organized in ways that show hierarchical and other types of relationships between words (such as in the classic *Roget's* thesaurus). In this case, the thesaurus will also include an alphabetical index of words to guide you to the proper entry.

Ready Reference Sources

The arrangement of print ready reference sources (such as almanacs, directories, quotation sources, guides, chronologies, and statistical sources) varies greatly according to the type of source. It may be alphabetical, chronological, or subject based. There will generally be at least one index, and sometimes more than one, to help readers find the information they seek.

Although the organization of reference sources may vary somewhat, your basic knowledge of the structure of books and of the concepts of alphanumeric organization, along with a willingness to read the preface or other introductory matter and to explore the available indexes, will allow you to navigate most print sources successfully. If a source seems confusing, take the time to stop for a moment and read through the introductory material that explains how to use it. This can actually save you lots of time (and frustration) in the long run.

SEARCHING IN ELECTRONIC DATABASES

Most electronic databases are also structured in fairly similar ways. This means that once we understand something about this basic structure, we can apply this understanding "across the board" in a number of different databases. And there are many different types of databases to consider, including these:

- Library catalogs, which list the books and other items held by particular libraries
- Bibliographic databases, which give publication information for articles, reports, and other types of materials
- Full-text databases, which take us a step further by including the full text of items
- Aggregated databases, which bring together the content of several different types of databases into one centralized, searchable location[2]

Generally speaking, these databases share a common kind of structure. They are all made up of **records;** each record is made up of a number of **fields;** each field contains searchable **data** (which explains why they're called databases).

Take, for example, the database ERIC, a bibliographic database (which also includes some full text) that's put out by the U.S. government. Here's part of a sample **record** from ERIC, for an article entitled "Literacy, Redefined" that appeared in *Library Journal* in September 2004:

ERIC #:	EJ706017
Title:	Literacy, Redefined
Authors:	Deane, Paul
Descriptors:	Professional Associations; Definitions; Writing Ability; Technological Literacy; Public Libraries; Reading Skills; Library Services; Adult Literacy; Literacy Education
Source:	Library Journal, v129 n14 p49 Sep 2004
Peer-Reviewed:	No
Publisher:	Library Journal, 360 Park Avenue South, New York, NY 10010. Tel: 800-588-1030 (Toll Free); Web site: http://www.libraryjournal.com.
Publication Date:	2004-09-01
Pages:	3
Pub Types:	Journal Articles; Reports - Descriptive
Abstract:	What does it mean to be literate in the 21st century? Fifty years ago a high school graduate with some basic reading and writing ability could get a well-paying blue-collar job. Today a person at the same level might have trouble finding good work and may be considered illiterate in some circles. The past half-century has brought us not only astonishing technological transformations but expanded definitions of the term literacy. While there is general agreement in 2004 that adult literacy is more than just a measure of basic reading skills, there is still no consensus on an exact definition. The American Library Association Committee on Literacy has drafted a document that offers 13 different definitions (available on www.ala.com). Minimalists define literacy as the basic set of skills required to function on a job--skills that include math and writing as well as reading. Others, arguing that the ability to use a computer is crucial to workplace productivity, have expanded the definition to incorporate technological literacy. While there is general agreement in 2004 that adult literacy is more than just a measure of basic reading skills, there is still no consensus on an exact definition. The American Library

Sample record from ERIC database (http://www.eric.ed.gov).

You can see the **fields** listed off to the left (ERIC #, title, authors, descriptors, source, etc.). Each of these fields holds **data** (the title "Literacy, Redefined," the name Paul Deane), which you can search for. The entire database is composed of more than a million records just like this, which have been entered over many years by people who looked at articles (or other materials) and decided what the title was, who the authors were, what descriptors (or subject headings) best described the content of the article, and so forth. Some of the records in ERIC also link to the full text of the publications described in the record.

When you search this database, you can choose to do a "keyword" search in multiple fields, or you can specify that you want to search in a particular field. Most databases have a "simple" or "basic" search mode:

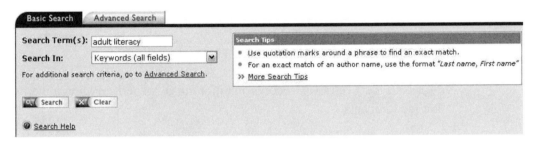

Basic search in ERIC database (http://www.eric.ed.gov).

as well as an "advanced" search mode where you can specify the exact fields to search, and easily limit searches by date of publication, language, etc.:

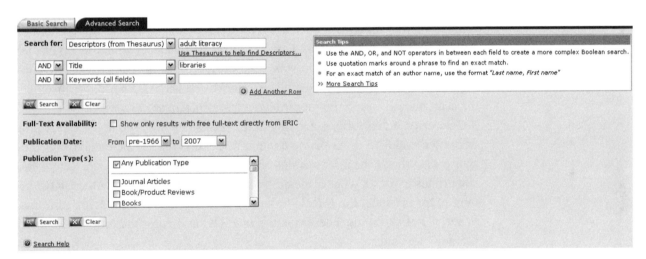

Advanced search in ERIC database (http://www.eric.ed.gov).

Furthermore, electronic databases generally offer the following options:[3]

- *The use of Boolean logic.* Boolean logic refers to our ability to combine search terms by using AND, OR, NOT—in order to broaden or narrow our searches in the database. This concept is often demonstrated with overlapping circles:

  dogs AND cats retrieves records that mention *both* terms

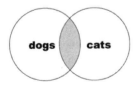

Boolean AND.

dogs OR cats retrieves records that mention *either* term

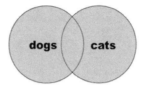

Boolean OR

dogs NOT cats retrieves records mentioning dogs and *excludes* records that mention cats

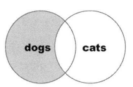

Boolean NOT.

- *Truncation or wild cards.* Truncation means replacing the letters at the end of a word with a symbol such as * or ? so that, for instance, *stereotyp** picks up *stereotype, stereotypes, stereotyping, stereotypical,* or any other possible endings. Wild card symbols may replace letters elsewhere in a word, for instance, the search term *wom?n* might retrieve the words *woman* or *women.*
- *A thesaurus.* A thesaurus is a listing of the terms that are used in the Descriptor or Subject fields to describe the content of documents for the database. A thesaurus also shows the relationships between Descriptors (or Subject terms) and sometimes explains what is meant by a particular Descriptor. In the ERIC database, for instance, the *ERIC Thesaurus* provides the official listing of terms. When we click on the Thesaurus tab in ERIC and enter the term "functional literacy" we find:

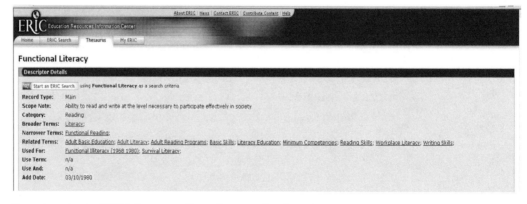

Sample entry in ERIC thesaurus (http://www.eric.ed.gov).

This entry defines the term for us (with a "scope note") and suggests broader, narrower, and related terms, all of which are used as Descriptors in ERIC. It also informs us that functional literacy is *used for* the terms **functional illiteracy** and **survival literacy** (in other words: these terms are not used as Descriptors in the database). As you can see, a thesaurus can be a wonderful tool for identifying which terms to use in your searches.

- *Proximity operators and nesting capabilities.* Although these terms sound intimidating, the concepts are actually very straightforward. AND, OR, and NOT, when used (as in the previous examples) to combine words, are called **Boolean operators. Proximity operators** allow you to specify how close together you want terms to be (that is, in what proximity to each other you want them to be). Many databases let you specify in this way:

    The letters **ADJ** (which stand for adjacent) allow you to locate one word followed by the next, for example, the search *bedtime ADJ story* retrieves records with the phrase *bedtime story.*

    Most databases now allow you to do this same search by putting the adjacent words in **quotation marks** so a search for *"bedtime story"* would also retrieve records with the phrase, *bedtime story.*

    The letter **W** (which stands for with) allows you to locate one word followed by the next, but to specify a certain number of words in–between; for example, the search *bedtime W3 story* will retrieve records with the word *bedtime* within three words of *story,* in that order (picking up phrases like *it's bedtime after a story* or *bedtime also means story time*).

    The letter **N** (which stands for near) allows you to locate one word within a certain number of words of another, in any order; for example, *bedtime N4 story* will retrieve records with the words bedtime and story within four words of each other, in any order (picking up phrases like *I'll tell you a story, then it's bedtime,* as well as *it's bedtime after a story*).

    Nesting capabilities allow you to group words together for your search. Systems will usually search for what's in parentheses first. So, if you want to find records in the database that mention bedtime stories about dogs or cats, you might search for *"bedtime stories" AND (dogs OR cats).* In this case, the system would first search for records that mentioned *dogs or cats,* then limit these to records that also included the phrase *bedtime stories.*

    If, instead, you searched for *"bedtime stories" AND dogs OR cats* instead (with no parentheses), the system would probably work across these Boolean commands from left to right, the same way you read a sentence. It would search for records with the phrase *bedtime stories,* then limit the search to records that also included the word *dogs* (following the "AND dogs" command), then go on to include all the records that mentioned *cats* (following the "OR cats" command). In this case, you might easily end up with a lot of records about cats that didn't mention bedtime stories at all!

- *A variety of output formats.* Most databases offer a brief and then a fuller view of each record. If a record looks good to you, you can usually "mark" it or "select" it in some way, and then, when you're done selecting records, you can choose to print, e-mail, or download the records. Many databases allow you to download the record in a certain bibliographic format such as MLA style or APA style.

In ERIC, for instance, we can mark records (like our "Literacy, Redefined" record) so that they are placed on a "clipboard." We can then choose to print, e-mail, or export them; or we can store them in the database for later use:

Output options in ERIC database (http://www.eric.ed.gov).

- *Search feedback.* Databases almost always tell you how many records were retrieved in each search, so that you can consider whether you might need to broaden or narrow the search. Some of them will also give you easy options to search within the results or limit your search in other ways, generate lists (or clusters) of the terms most commonly used in the records you've retrieved, or even suggest alternative spellings. All of these features are designed to help you evaluate the search results and, if necessary, "try, try again!"

Different databases offer different interfaces, with variations on the available search options. Just as you would read the preface to a new print reference book, leaf through the table of contents, and check out the indexes, when you encounter a new (or a newly refurbished) database, you should feel free to click on the "About" link to learn more about the content; check out the "Search Tips" to learn what search options are available to you, and never hesitate to make use of the "Help" screens when you feel confused. Most database producers work hard to provide useful information and support on these screens, so why not use them? Online tutorials have also been developed for many databases providing yet another way for us to learn more.

From the Structure to the Search

Having reviewed the structure of electronic databases and having considered some of the search options available, let's give some thought to how we would actually go about performing a search (the all important "part three" of the reference interview). To perform an effective search in an online database, search experts Geraldene Walker and Joseph Janes suggest following these eight steps:[4]

1. *Listen* to, or read, your patron's query, and be sure you understand it (remember: question negotiation may need to occur before you can actually begin to search). This is also the moment at which you might start thinking about which database(s) to search.

2. Identify the major *concepts* in the query. These are the basic ideas underlying your patron's information need.

3. Identify potential *terms* to correspond to those concepts. You can brainstorm some keywords for searching; you may also want to consult a thesaurus if the database offers one.

4. Select alternative (*narrower, broader, related*) *terms* to use if the original strategy needs help; consider whether it would make sense to *truncate* any of the search terms.

5. Determine logical (*Boolean*) *relationships* between terms. Are there synonyms or related terms you should combine using OR to broaden your search? Are there terms you should combine using AND to narrow or focus the search? Are there any terms you absolutely need to exclude (using NOT)?

6. Begin the *search*. This is where you get to try out your search in one or more databases.

7. *Examine* a few records. Really look at them; what keywords appear in those that seem especially relevant? What descriptors or subject headings are attached to the records?

8. *Revise* and *refine* your search based on these initial results. If you have too few results, what are some ways you could broaden your search? If you have too many, how might you narrow it? If there are a few good items, but most seem a little off, how might you refocus your search to improve it?

This final step, revising and refining until you get a good, solid set of results, is the mark of the true professional. There are several tricks of the trade you can use to broaden and narrow your searches.

"Pearl growing" is one such technique. It involves identifying at least one useful or relevant item (the "pearl"), carefully examining that record for descriptors and keywords, and then plugging those terms into the database in the hopes of retrieving additional relevant records.

If you have very few records, you can also revisit the list of potential terms (from step 3) and try out some new ones. Check the thesaurus again for related or broader terms; you can use the word OR to add them to your latest search. If you're searching in specific fields (such as the Descriptor field), try searching as a Keyword (this generally looks in the descriptor, title, and abstract fields); or you can even try searching the Full Text of documents (this is an option in many databases).

On the other hand, if you have too many records, you may want to restrict your search to using official descriptors and searching *only* in the Descriptor field, especially if many of the initial results seem off-base. The thesaurus may be key here in helping you choose precise search terms. You can also add additional terms to your search (using AND) to focus it more appropriately. This last technique is sometimes known as the "building block approach."[5] And you might consider limiting your search in other ways, for example, by date (including only very recent items) or language (including only items published in English).

Database search options grow more sophisticated each day. Many databases now offer choices for natural language searching and relevance ranking of search results (much like Internet search engines); some allow you the option to find "more like these"; some cluster sets of results visually. But it is still useful to know and practice the basic search techniques described here, which allow you to tap into the contents of online databases and extract relevant material.

SEARCHING THE WEB

The Internet is a global system of interconnected networks through which people are able to communicate using different protocols: sending e-mails, transferring files, accessing databases, and viewing and manipulating files that are located on remote computers. One of the most important protocols, HTTP (hypertext transfer protocol) was developed in the late 1980s by Tim Berners-Lee. HTTP revolutionized the Internet by allowing files of various types (text, images, sound) on different computers to be linked to each other in an almost seamless fashion; thus, the World Wide Web was born. The first graphical Web browser (Mosaic) premiered a few years later in 1993, making the Web easy to use. Now, in the twenty-first century, use of the Web has become ubiquitous in the United States, especially for those who work in libraries. So much of our activity on the Internet is accomplished by using a Web browser (such as Netscape, Internet Explorer, or Firefox) that we often use the terms *Internet* and *Web* interchangeably.

Some people think of the World Wide Web as a giant, searchable database of Web pages. In reality, it is much more complicated than this. For one thing, "pages" of text and images make up only a portion of what's on the Web. It includes a huge diversity of materials, including streaming videos, podcasts, newsfeeds, and pages that are dynamically generated by databases for brief periods of time. Also, unlike the electronic databases discussed previously, whose content is, for the most part, carefully controlled and classified, the Web is a wild mixture of sources of all shapes, sizes and formats, with no external controls and little in the way of "classification." It evolves constantly, so only a certain percentage of the information that's on the Web ever gets indexed, and what is there today may well be gone tomorrow. The search tools we use to find information on the Web, however, are evolving right alongside it. Some useful types of search engines and directories help us make our way through the glorious, treacherous Web and (sometimes) retrieve exactly what we need.

Search engines are programs that enable us to search the Web. They have three major components:[6]

1. "Crawlers," or "spiders," that traverse the Web gathering information—visiting Web pages, reading them, and following the links on the pages to additional pages. They return periodically to check for changes.
2. An index, or catalog, that contains copies of the Web pages located by the crawlers. It can take a while for new or altered Web pages to be found by the crawlers and added to the index.
3. Search engine software that sorts through the Web pages, matches them to queries, and ranks them by relevance (using highly sophisticated algorithms).

The collection, indexing, and ranking methods vary from search engine to search engine (as do the interfaces). The ranking algorithms, in particular, are closely guarded secrets. They take into account factors such as the location of words on a page, the frequency of words, how many links are made to a page by other pages, and how many users click on a page when it comes up in a search. Most search engines also take into account the use of *meta-tags*, descriptive information and keywords that are not visible when we're viewing pages on the Web, but that can be added to the "backside" of a Web page to provide additional information to search engines (sort of like cataloging a book for retrieval in an online catalog).

The major search engines are constantly evolving, speeding up their collection processes, expanding their indexes, and tweaking their ranking algorithms. Google's system for ranking pages, for instance, reportedly takes into account more than 200 different factors to help sort through and rank the tens of billions of Web pages stored in its indexes.[7]

Librarians Myrtle Bolner and Gayle Poirier offer a useful, if somewhat artificial, way to categorize the types of search engines that we commonly use in libraries:[8]

- *General (or keyword) search engines* offer broad coverage of the Web, with basic and advanced keyword search options. These are what we typically think of when we hear the term *search engine*—search tools like Google, Yahoo!, Live Search, and Ask.com.
- *Meta-search engines* simultaneously run their queries against multiple search engines and bring back the top results to a single place. Prominent examples of meta-search engines include Dogpile, Clusty, Kartoo, and Mamma.
- *Subject search engines* search specific portions of the Web and are useful for focusing in on subject- or discipline-specific types of information. Examples include FindLaw.com (for legal information), USA.gov (for government information), and scirus.com (for scientific information).
- *Directories* involve the classification of information into categories by human beings (although all of the major directories now have search engines on their sites as well). Some useful general directories are the Open Directory Project (dmoz.org), the Yahoo! Directory (dir.yahoo.com), and Infomine (infomine.ucr.edu). A number of excellent directories of reference sources also exist; these are discussed in more detail in Chapter 9.

It's sometimes hard to make clear distinctions among the types of search engines, as the major "players" now offer multiple kinds of search options. For instance, Yahoo! started life as a directory, but its keyword search engine is now at least as important (if not more important) to its users. Google, known for being a general keyword search engine, also offers a directory and a subject-specific search option for U.S. government information. Most of these search engines offer subareas where you can search specifically for news, images, audio, video, or blogs. Still, it's useful to consider these major types of search tools that are available to us.

Using Search Engines

One of the most attractive features of a search engine like Google is its apparent simplicity. The empty search box at google.com sits ready, waiting for you to enter a word, a set of words, or a phrase, and click on the "Google search" button. In the blink of an eye, the search engine returns hundreds, thousands, or even millions of links to Web pages, carefully ranked, so that (theoretically) the most relevant links are at the top of the list.

Google search screen, Trademark of Google, Inc.

Of course, we know that the situation is more complex than the simple search box would have us believe. Because the Web is so vast and because people have such a wide variety of information needs, even the best ranking algorithm cannot always ensure that the most relevant links will rise to the top. Web searches sometimes require more thought and planning than the average user might think, and the creators of the search engines know that. This is where your reference interview skills, as well as your search skills, come into play.

Just beyond the alluringly simple search box, Advanced Search options await you (at all of the major search engines). As a matter of fact, the options you have for searching are similar to some of the options available in online databases, and so your database search skills will serve you well. In most search engines you can use AND (or +) to include all terms; NOT (or –) to exclude certain terms; OR to include alternative terms; and quotation marks (" ") to search for an exact phrase. The major search engines all have advanced search features that allow you to search particular fields (such as the title field or URL) and to limit your results to pages written in specific languages, updated after a certain date, belonging to a certain domain (such as .gov, .com, or .edu), etc. For a quick guide to the features of some major search engines, see Greg Notess's "Search Engine Features" chart at http://searchengineshowdown.com/features/.[9]

Google Advanced Search Screen, Trademark of Google, Inc.

Internet search engines are designed to support our casual searches for information and library patrons often won't turn to you for assistance until they've spent quite some time searching the Web on their own. To be prepared to help them, you should:

- Become *very* familiar with the major keyword search engines (these currently include Google, Yahoo!, Live Search, and Ask.com).

  - Study and use their "Advanced Search" options.
  - Check their "Help" pages to see what their search rules are.

- If your favorite search engine fails you, try others.

  - Remember, a meta-search engine can help you search several at once.
  - Or, a subject-specific search engine might bring unexpected sites to the top of the search results.

- Take some time to play with new features and try out new search engines on a regular basis.

Fortunately, the major search engines are eager to keep you abreast of new developments. You can subscribe to corporate blogs from Google (http://googleblog. blogspot.com/), Yahoo! (http://www.ysearchblog.com/), Live Search (http://blogs. msdn.com/livesearch/), and Ask.com (http://blog.ask.com/). Other sites worth visiting, most of which feature free e-mail newsletters and/or blogs, include Search Engine Watch (http://searchenginewatch.com/), ResearchBuzz (http://www.researchbuzz. org), and Pandia Search Central (http://www.pandia.com/).

The Limits of Web Search Engines

The Web is a tremendous resource for reference librarians, and search engines help us sort through the massive amounts of information that it makes available to us. It's important to bear in mind, however, that *not everything is available on the Web*. Even with recent book digitization projects underway by Google, Microsoft, and Yahoo!,[10] much valuable information is still only available in our libraries in nondigital formats. Furthermore, lots of information that is in digital format and is available on the Web is not readily accessible through Web search engines. This includes information stored in many databases (especially subscription databases), information that is dynamically generated, information on sites that block Web crawlers, information on pages that are not linked to other pages, and very new information (unless it's fed to search engines or otherwise automatically indexed). Researchers have calculated that this "deep Web" or "invisible Web" is much larger than the indexed Web (possibly hundreds of times larger).[11]

It's important to remember that Web search engines tap into resources whose depth and quality vary wildly: anyone from a bright 5-year-old interested in stars to a physicist who specializes in superclusters of galaxies can put up a Web page. Most library databases and print sources are subject to editorial controls; database vendors and libraries have established guidelines to determine what they do and do not include in their collections. This is not at all true for general search engines, which tap indiscriminately into the broad range of resources on the Web. Librarians and their patrons must carefully evaluate the Web pages returned, assessing their accuracy, authority, currency, content, and organization. This process is sometimes difficult and can be extremely time consuming; in some cases, a search in a print source or library database may be faster and more efficient. For these reasons, it's vital for us to know how to search print resources and library databases as well as the Web in an effective manner and to stand ready, willing, and able to use appropriate search tools in any given situation.

IN SUM

Searching for information is a key component of reference work. By familiarizing yourself with the most common organizational schemes of print sources; understanding the structure of online databases and their basic search options; and carefully studying, as well as playing with, the major search engines, you can be well prepared to assist patrons as they search for information. It takes a while to develop an understanding of what the different types of information sources have to offer, and to learn how to search them effectively; sometimes it may seem like just when you've completely mastered a source, a new edition (or interface, or search function) comes along that makes you feel like a beginner all over again! Luckily, such changes are usually gradual and incremental. By building upon the knowledge you already possess, you will be able to stay current and to adeptly navigate your way through a variety of sources in search of information.

REVIEW

1. One of your patrons (a college student) is looking for material that connects *skipping school* to *drug and alcohol abuse*. She is mostly interested in recent research. Using ERIC, can you find her at least 10 relevant resources published since 1995? Use the thesaurus to find appropriate descriptors, use Boolean connectors, and try revising your search based on your initial results.

2. Try finding relevant material on the same topic using one of the major search engines. Make use of the advanced search features, either on the Advanced Search screen or using appropriate symbols and connectors. What advantages does Web searching hold over ERIC, and what are its limitations?

NOTES

1. Samuel Johnson, as quoted in Boswell, J. (1791). *Boswell's Life of Johnson*. Project Gutenberg edition available online at http://www.gutenberg.org/etext/1564
2. Bolner, M. S., and Poirier, G. A. (2007). *The research process: Books & beyond* (4th ed). Dubuque, IA: Kendall/Hunt, p. 59.
3. List adapted from Walker, G. & Janes, J. (1999). *Online retrieval: A dialogue of theory and practice*. Englewood, CO: Libraries Unlimited, p. 52.
4. ibid, chapter 6.
5. Dalrymple, P. W. (2001). Bibliographic control, organization of information, and search strategies. In R. E. Bopp & L. C. Smith (Eds.), *Reference and information services: An introduction* (3rd ed., pp. 69–96). Englewood, CO: Libraries Unlimited.
6. Sullivan, D. (2007, March 14). How search engines work. Available online at http://searchenginewatch.com/showPage.html?page=2168031
7. Hansell, S. (2007, June 3). Google keeps tweaking its search engine. *New York Times*. Available online at http://www.nytimes.com
8. Bolner & Poirier, *The research process*, p. 134.
9. Notess, G. R. (2006). Search engine features. Available online at Search Engine Showdown: The Users' Guide to Web Searching: http://searchengineshowdown.com/features
10. To explore further, visit Google Book Search (http://books.google.com), Live Search Books (http://books.live.com), and Open Content Alliance (http://www.opencontentalliance.org).
11. For more information on the "deep web" or "invisible web" see: The 'deep' Web: Surfacing hidden value (2001), available online at http://www.brightplanet.com/technology/deepweb.asp, and Zillman, M. P. (2004), Deep Web research, available online at http://www.llrx.com/features/deepweb.htm

CHAPTER 5

Finding Books: Library Catalogs and Bibliographies

A catalog is a labor-saving device in library work. From it both reader and attendant can ascertain whether the library has a certain book. By consulting the catalog for the class-number, the book may be looked for in its proper place, thus often saving hunting through the shelves in several classes.[1]

When you ask people for the first word that comes to mind when they think about libraries, their response will probably be: *Books.*[2] For better or for worse, the idea of the library is closely tied to the idea of books. The very word *library* is derived from *liber,* a Latin word for "book."[3] Uniting people with the books they want and need is an important part of librarianship.

Because so many people come to the library in search of books, the library catalog is quite possibly the single most useful reference tool you have at your disposal. The catalog is an ingenious device that provides access to individual items in library collections, not just books, but also CDs, DVDs, and (in some cases) online items such as e-books or government publications. Today's online catalogs can be searched in many ways; it is important for you to master these and to become an expert in the use of your catalog. Fortunately, this shouldn't be difficult, as most librarians get lots and lots of practice looking for items in their catalogs!

In addition to discussing library catalogs and how to search them, this chapter also briefly touches on the benefits of several other book-finding tools: union catalogs, trade bibliographies, and subject bibliographies.

THE LIBRARY CATALOG

The humble library catalog has a long history. The first known listing of books, written on a Sumerian clay tablet, is more than 4,000 years old. Through the millennia, libraries have kept track of their holdings using papyrus, wax tablets, handwritten lists in books, printed catalogs, and card catalogs.[4] As the format evolved, so did the function; gradually, the catalog grew into a highly sophisticated finding tool. The catalog most commonly found in U.S. libraries today is the Web-based OPAC, or Online Public Access Catalog.

A library catalog is basically a collection of records representing items in the library's collections. The catalog allows library patrons and staff to find items in the collection by searching it in various ways. Those of us old enough to remember the traditional card catalogs that flourished in libraries before the 1980s probably remember that we could look up books (and other items) by Author, Title, or Subject. Online catalogs still allow us to search by author, title and subject; they also allow us to search by keyword, call number, and a number of other access points. In addition, the online catalog offers us the options of combining words and limiting searches in important ways, of linking to related records, and of browsing by subject or call number area.

AN EXAMPLE: THE ARKANSAS STATE LIBRARY CATALOG

As an example, let's consider the catalog of the Arkansas State Library available on the Web at http://arkstar.asl.lib.ar.us/. This particular catalog uses software from the SirsiDynix corporation; other popular library catalogs are put out by Endeavor Information Systems, Innovative Interfaces, Ex Libris, and The Library Corporation, among others. Each type of catalog has its own special options and qualities; however, the features described here are fairly standard.

Author, Title, Subject . . . and More!

First, note the access points for searching this catalog in its "basic search" mode.

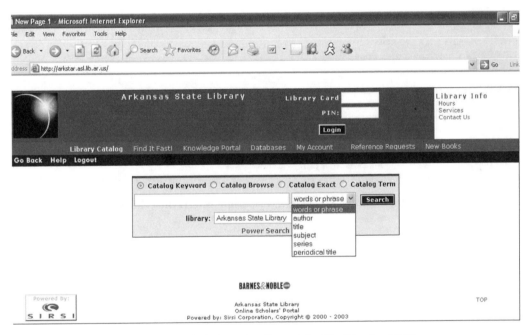

Screenshot used by permission of SirsiDynix. Copyright SirsiDynix, 2007.

Patrons can immediately choose to search the catalog by Keyword ("word or phrase"), Author, Title, Subject, Series title, or Periodical title.

A search—on the subject *Gardening,* for instance—yields a number of records for books and other items (such as online government documents).

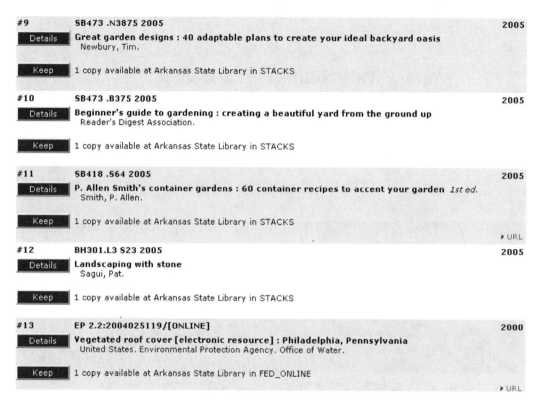

Screenshot used by permission of SirsiDynix. Copyright SirsiDynix, 2007.

Clicking on the Details for any given item leads to richer item information and a catalog record.

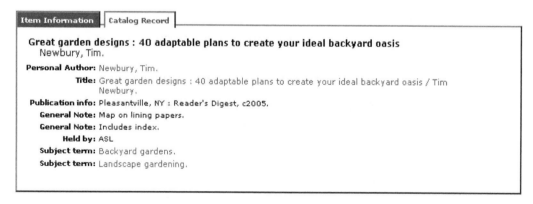

Screenshot used by permission of SirsiDynix. Copyright SirsiDynix, 2007.

Each of the fields in blue is also hyperlinked, allowing people to easily search for items by the same author, or on the same subject.

The "Power Search" in the catalog gives patrons the option to combine terms (using the Boolean connectors AND, OR, and NOT) and to limit searches by library, language, format, item type, location, etc.

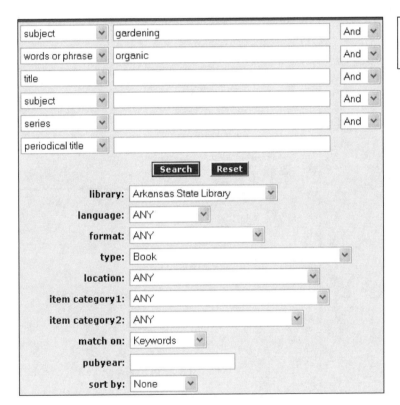

Screenshot used by permission of SirsiDynix. Copyright SirsiDynix, 2007.

Many catalogs, including this one, also suggest appropriate alternate search terms and allow users to "link out" to other databases or search engines to try their searches there (see the link to Google and suggestions for searching, in the panel below and to the left):

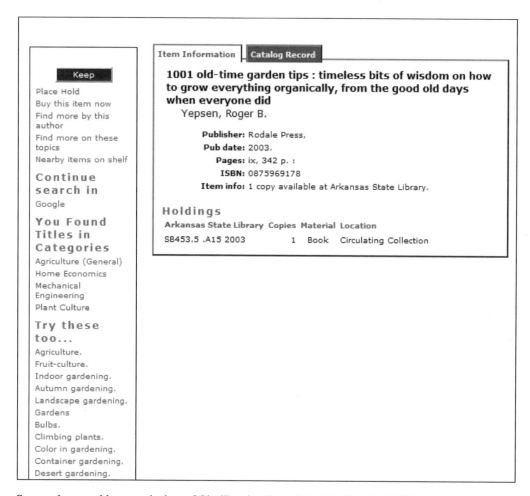

Screenshot used by permission of SirsiDynix. Copyright SirsiDynix, 2007.

UNION CATALOGS

Long ago, librarians figured out that if they could share records for books and other materials, rather than creating records from scratch for every item that came into the library, their workloads would be much lighter. From the early 1900s on, many libraries purchased catalog cards from the Library of Congress. The Library of Congress also created a print National Union Catalog, so that libraries could see where a book might be located if they did not own it themselves.

OCLC WorldCat

Over the course of the twentieth century, as computers became more commonplace and networks started to grow, some libraries began to systematically pool their cataloging efforts. Perhaps the most successful cooperative catalog in the world began in the late 1960s, when several college libraries in Ohio came together to create OCLC, a regional computer system for sharing resources.[5] Today, OCLC (the Online Computer Library Center) serves libraries in more than 100 countries and territories around the world, offering cataloging tools and a variety of databases. Their most important database is the mammoth WorldCat, an online catalog of 75 million records that reflects the holdings of more than 40,000 participating libraries and greatly facilitates interlibrary loan. WorldCat is available at http://firstsearch.oclc.org; access requires a login and password from participating libraries. A simpler version is available for free at http://www.worldcat.org.

In many ways, WorldCat works just like any other library catalog. You can search by author, title, subject, keyword, or various combinations of these; you can do simple searches or advanced searches, view brief records or fuller records, and link to records that are related in some way to the one you are viewing. But WorldCat is special in a couple of ways. As a union catalog, it shows not only what's available at your library, but also lists "Libraries worldwide that own item."

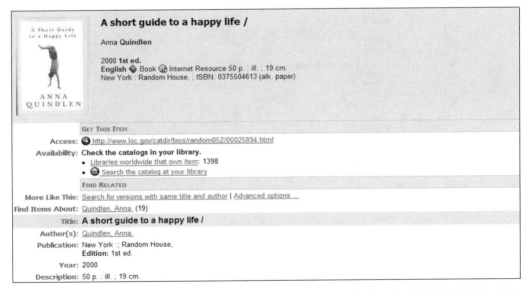

From OCLC's WorldCat database. Information used with permission of OCLC. WorldCat® is a registered trademark of OCLC Online Computer Library Center, Inc.

If you click on this "Libraries worldwide" link, you get a list of these libraries, along with a link to their catalogs; some libraries will allow you to request items on interlibrary loan directly through WorldCat.

The free version of WorldCat (Open WorldCat, available at http://www.worldcat. org) automatically displays libraries where the book is available, arranged by distance from your zip code. And OCLC is working to make libraries' holdings easily available to people doing searches in Google or Yahoo!: entering *"find in a library"* in a Google search, or *site:worldcatlibraries.org* in Yahoo!, will take you to a WorldCat record in the free version of the catalog (for a selected subset of books). Give it a try!

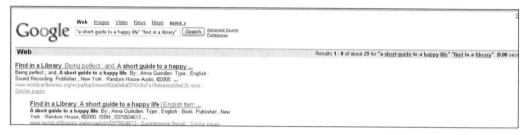

Google search, Trademark of Google, Inc.

Clicking on the second link leads to this search result.

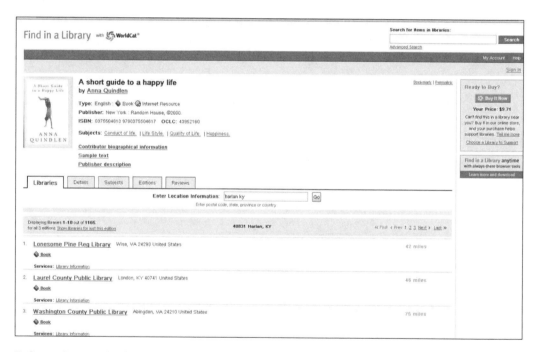

Information used with permission of OCLC. WorldCat® is a registered trademark of OCLC Online Computer Library Center, Inc.

State and Regional Union Catalogs

Many states and regions offer union catalogs on a smaller scale in an effort to show which libraries in a *particular area* own items. Some of these union catalogs are spin-offs from WorldCat including the Alaska Library Network Catalog, the Idaho Statewide Catalog, the Montana Library Network group catalog, and the Statewide Illinois Library Catalog. See http://www.worldcat.org/sitesandtips/ for a full listing (and try one out!).

Other state and regional catalogs use their own systems. For instance, in Iowa, the SILO Locator, at http://z3950.silo.lib.ia.us/cgi-bin/zform.CGI?SILO allows you to search the holdings of public, state, academic, and special libraries throughout the state of Iowa.

Screenshot used with permission of the State Library of Iowa, 2007.

And here is the search result.

Screenshot used with permission of the State Library of Iowa, 2007.

TRADE BIBLIOGRAPHIES: WHAT'S FOR SALE?

It could be that a patron wishes to purchase a book; having read it, he or she now wants to own it. Or perhaps someone has requested that you purchase a particular book for the collection.

For many years, *Books in Print* (available by subscription at http://www.booksinprint.com) was the standard tool used in libraries to find the price of a book, whether it was currently available, and who the publisher was. *Books in Print* offers a database of more than 5 million searchable books, audio books, and videos, including materials that are in print, out of print, and forthcoming. You can search the database in multiple ways and create lists of items you are interested in acquiring. For many titles there are chapter previews, professional reviews, and biographical information about the author.

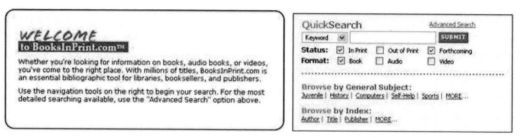

Screenshot from Bowker's BookInPrint.com.™ © Copyright 2008. R.R. Bowker LLC. Used with permission. Books In Print is a registered trademark of R.R. Bowker LLC.

Recently, the freely available Amazon.com has given *Books in Print* stiff competition. Many libraries use Amazon.com to check pricing and bibliographic information, preview title information, and read editorial reviews and reviews written by customers. As a huge commercial database, Amazon.com naturally allows the creation and management of shopping lists; in addition to books, it includes music CDs, DVDs, and a growing assortment of consumer products (everything from electronics to house wares to groceries).

SUBJECT BIBLIOGRAPHIES

A final type of bibliography that merits discussion is the *subject bibliography*. Subject bibliographies are lists of material that someone has compiled about a certain topic or individual. Subject bibliographies may or may not be annotated (including brief descriptions and sometimes evaluations of the items on the list). They may be very broad in scope or they may be limited to a specific time period, format, and so on.

Subject bibliographies can show up in magazines or journals; many serious book-length subject bibliographies have been compiled. There is even an index devoted to helping people find bibliographies (H.W. Wilson's *Bibliographic Index*).

To see if your library has a book-length bibliography on a particular subject, you can simply go into the library catalog, select a *Subject* search, and enter the subject you are searching for, plus the word *bibliography*. For instance, if you wanted to find a bibliography on Miami, Florida, you could do a Subject search for *Miami* and *Bibliography* and you might retrieve Susan Weiss's 1995 work, *Miami Bibliography* (published by the Historical Association of Southern Florida). You can view the full record for this bibliography at http://www.worldcatlibraries.org/oclc/35369778 and, because this book has been digitized, you can even click on purl.fcla.edu within the record to see what the full text looks like (remembering, of course, that the organization of subject bibliographies will vary according to topic).

IN SUM

Many patrons will come to your library looking for books. By skillfully searching your OPAC, along with modern online union catalogs such as WorldCat, you can help them locate just about any book they are interested in and even help them find it for sale if they wish. Should they need more books on a particular subject, a subject bibliography can make an excellent complement to the catalog.

REVIEW

1. Spend some "quality time" playing with your OPAC. What options does your OPAC provide for sorting or limiting the results of a search? Does it suggest further searches or "link out" to external resources?
2. What is WorldCat, and how can it be useful to your library?
3. A patron is looking for *Tennis for Dummies,* but it is not in your library. Can you quickly help him find a library that does have it? He is thinking of buying it; can you tell him how much it might cost?
4. A high school student is doing an ambitious project on women in Muslim countries. Can you help her find resources in your library? Can you use World-Cat to find a book-length bibliography of sources in English on this topic?

NOTES

1. Dana, J. C. (1903). *A library primer* (3rd ed). Chicago: Library Bureau, p. 94.
2. OCLC Online Computer Library Center. (2005). *Perceptions of libraries and information resources.* Dublin, OH: OCLC. Available online at http://www.oclc.org/reports/2005perceptions.htm. pp. 3–31.
3. *Oxford English Dictionary.* (2007). Oxford, England: Oxford University Press. Available online at http://www.oed.com
4. Taylor, A. (1999). *The organization of information.* Englewood, CO: Libraries Unlimited.
5. *History of OCLC.* (2007). Available online at http://www.oclc.org/about/history/default.htm

CHAPTER 6

Finding Articles: Indexes and Databases

Three hostile newspapers are more to be feared than a thousand bayonets.[1]

When you think of the word *index,* the first image that probably comes to mind is that alphabetical listing at the end of a book, the one that tells you where subjects appear in the text of the book. Or perhaps you picture your index finger, the finger you use to navigate through the words in that alphabetical listing.

The periodical indexes in libraries also serve as navigational tools. Traditionally, a periodical index was a listing of the subjects and authors of periodical articles, that is, articles appearing in magazines, journals, and newspapers. A searcher would look in an index under a particular author's name, or a subject, and find the title of an article either written by that person or about that subject. The index also provided enough information to let you know which periodical it appeared in, and where.

GENERAL PERIODICAL INDEXES

Among the oldest periodical indexes is the *Reader's Guide to Periodical Literature,* published by the H. W. Wilson Company, a staple in libraries of all sorts for many years, dating back to 1901. You may remember its green volumes from the libraries of your youth. It covered approximately 150 magazines; when you looked up a subject, such as Player Pianos or Food, Frozen, you would find a handy list of articles about that topic, appearing in some of those magazines.

Someone interested in women's health in 1953 could, by checking the *Reader's Guide* under the subject heading *Women—Health and hygiene,* learn of an article from *Science Digest* with the intriguing title, "Nervous woman of the machine age." In the same period, the topic *Television—Political uses* would provide citations to articles such as "Television, a new campaign weapon" (*The New Republic*) and "Politicos learn how to act" (*Life*). Checking the index for March 1967–February 1968 for *Youth—United States* would point the curious to questions such as "What's the matter with the younger generation?" (*Reader's Digest*) and investigations of "Our mysterious children" (*Saturday Evening Post*).

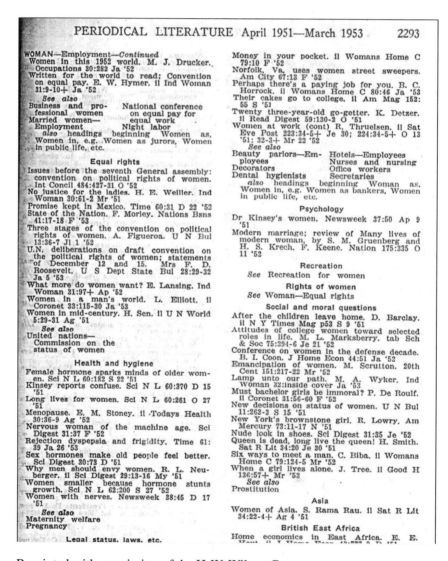

Reprinted with permission of the H. W. Wilson Company.

You can imagine how useful, and necessary, this kind of finding tool was, even in the days when we generally had access to a much smaller number of magazines and journals. Not only did such a tool serve to bring together articles on a single subject (or by a single author) that might have appeared in many different magazines, it also cumulated on an annual basis, so that you might find items that appeared on that subject last year, or the year before that, or 10 years ago.

The *Reader's Guide* was just one of many periodical indexes available to libraries. Many libraries subscribed to other, more specialized indexes, such as the *Humanities Index,* the *Social Sciences Index,* or the *Book Review Index.* Some indexes, often the more scholarly ones, included brief abstracts (or summaries) of articles and bore the title *Abstracts:* for instance, *Psychological Abstracts,* or *Biological Abstracts.* The arrangement within the abstracts was sometimes a bit different, but the idea was the same: to provide access to the articles contained in magazines or journals.

Beginning as early as the 1960s, producers of some indexes began to computerize their operations and to make information directly searchable by clients over the computer (for a fee). In the 1970s and 1980s, many libraries began to offer online searching for their patrons by dialing into databases that were maintained and made accessible by companies such as DIALOG and BRS. These searches were expensive; there were charges for every search, for every record viewed, and for every record printed. You had to know specific search commands to search the databases, but (as discussed in Chapter 4) having access to the contents of these indexes in online databases allowed people to search them in many additional ways: by keyword, by title of the magazine, and so on. In some cases, you could even access the full text of an article.

In the mid-1980s, a company called InfoTrac began to market an exciting new product to libraries: an index to periodicals on CD-ROM. It had a friendly interface, with a menu that allowed for easy searching by the library patron. Patrons could reiterate searches as many times as needed, without incurring additional costs. The idea of making periodical indexes available on CD-ROM was a tremendous hit. Soon most periodical indexes were migrating to CD-ROM format.

In the 1990s, as the use of the Internet became widespread, periodical indexes made another leap: from CD-ROM to the Web. Today, almost all libraries subscribe to Web-based periodical indexes and abstracts to help their patrons locate articles on particular topics, or perhaps to track down that one specific article they remember reading sometime last year. The Web-based indexes are clearly superior to their print counterparts in many ways: searching is easier, faster, and more flexible, and there are links to the full text of the magazine and journal articles in many cases. A handful of companies (Wilson, Gale, ProQuest, EBSCO, LexisNexis, OCLC) produce most of the databases, so that many of the interfaces look similar to each other.

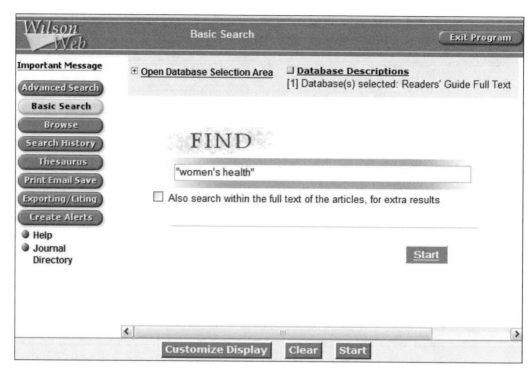

Screenshot reprinted with permission of the H. W. Wilson Company.

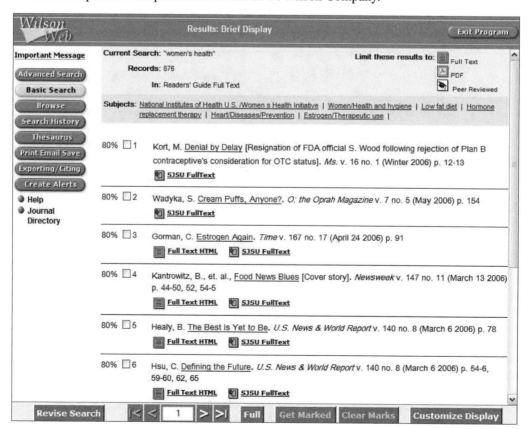

Screenshot reprinted with permission of the H. W. Wilson Company.

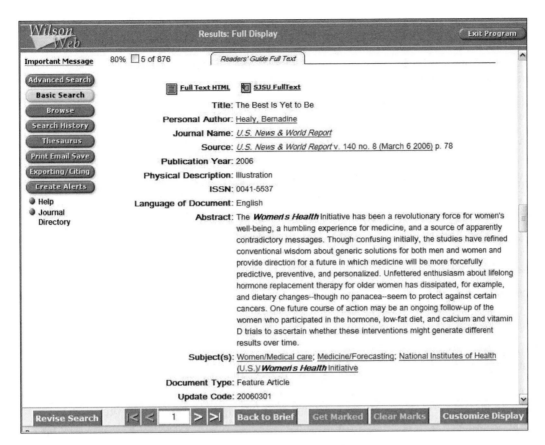

Screenshot reprinted with permission of the H. W. Wilson Company.

Some users complain that it isn't as easy to browse through a Web-based index as it is with a print version. But for the most part, the usefulness of the electronic indexes is unquestionably greater, and many libraries have dropped subscriptions to their print indexes in favor of their electronic counterparts.[2] Still, in many cases online coverage goes back only to the 1980s (or 1960s at the earliest). Oftentimes an additional subscription is required for retrospective coverage; for example, *Reader's Guide* offers *Reader's Guide Retrospective,* which covers periodicals back into the 1890s. By holding on to their older print indexes, librarians ensure that their patrons will have the ability to access articles in older magazines and journals without paying for an additional subscription.

Reader's Guide has been given here as a prominent example of a periodical database because of its age. Produced by the H. W. Wilson company, it covers more than 400 magazines and journals of a popular nature, going back to 1983; about half of them are available in full-text for recent years, in some cases as far back as 1994. There are many other excellent *general* periodical databases as well, most of which include a surprising amount of scholarly material.[3]

EBSCO's *Academic Search Premier* indexes more than 8,000 publications, more than half of them in full-text, and primarily scholarly journals from a variety of disciplines. It also includes about 900 general-interest periodicals; dates vary by title, with coverage of some (many of which are full-text) going back to 1975.

Expanded Academic ASAP, provided by Gale, carries citations for more than 3,300 periodicals, more than 2,000 of which are full-text, with indexing going back to 1980 for some titles (e.g., *Architectural Digest, Golf Magazine*). Gale also offers *Infotrac OneFile,* which combines several of its other indexes to cover more than 10,000 titles in magazines, journals, and lots of newspapers and newswires, more than half of them in full-text. Dates of coverage are similar to those of *Expanded Academic ASAP.*

ProQuest Research Library indexes more than 3,500 periodicals, with more than two-thirds provided full-text. Coverage for some titles (such as *Money*) reaches back to the early 1970s, although the mid-1990s is more typical. Libraries can customize their subscriptions by adding modules focusing on particular topics such as health, women's interest, business, and so on, to a core set of more than 800 periodicals.

LexisNexis Academic carries the full text of more than 6,000 publications. Although LexisNexis is perhaps best known for its coverage of legal materials, it also provides a large number of general-interest periodicals such as *Consumer Reports, The Economist,* and *Newsweek.*

Google and Microsoft now offer free searches for scholarly articles in their search engines by using *Google Scholar* (http://scholar.google.com) and *Live Search Academic* (http://academic.live.com). These specialized search engines offer a convenient way to identify articles from many scholarly publications. Full text of the articles is *sometimes* freely available (and if your library subscribes to a full-text database, you *may* be able to link seamlessly to the full text of articles). Coverage and indexing, however, are hit-or-miss, especially when compared to the carefully controlled indexes listed previously.

NEWSPAPER INDEXES

In addition to "general" periodical indexes that cover a variety of magazines and journals, newspaper indexes are an important type of index for libraries to offer. In many towns and cities, the public library has long been *the* place that has archived copies of the local newspaper for posterity, and in some cases even indexed them. Also, many reference librarians have traditionally maintained clippings files of articles from local newspapers on topics of interest to the community.

Much of this indexing activity has of course become computerized and in many cases has migrated to the Web (along with many newspapers). Many newspapers, even in smaller towns, now have a Web presence. Take, for example, the *Winchester Sun* of Winchester Kentucky (a community of 16,000 people). The newspaper has a solid Web site at http://www.winchestersun.com/, with free access to articles and a searchable archive that goes back for 6 months. The *Vevay Reveille-Enterprise* and *Switzerland Democrat,* from Vevay, Indiana (with a population of just over 1,700 people) is another example. Their site at http://www.vevaynewspapers.com/ requires registration for access and searching, but online registration is free. Print newspapers are still going strong in many communities; a good free index for a number of small local papers whose contents have been scanned and put on the Web is available at SmallTownPapers.com.

Larger newspapers, of course, are also widely available on the Web. An excellent general listing of online newspapers (published in the United States and other countries as well) is available at http://www.onlinenewspapers.com/. Just like their small town counterparts, newspapers serving larger communities may have limited information available online, portions of the newspaper that are available *only* in print, limited archives, and may require registration (which may or may not be free). For instance, the *Wall Street Journal* (http://online.wsj.com) makes some articles freely available on their Web site, but the full text of many articles is available only to subscribers. The illustrious *New York Times* (http://www.nytimes.com) boasts a beautiful Web site, with a searchable archive back to 1851 and free full-text articles from 1987 to the present and 1851–1922. Even the *Times*, however, charges a fee for articles written before 1987 which are not in the public domain.

Thus, the Web site of the newspaper itself is not always the best place to search for a specific article, even if the Web site has an excellent archive, unless you are a subscriber or are prepared to pay up front. But note: your library may already subscribe to a periodical database that indexes newspapers and picks up the full text of older articles. *The New York Times,* for instance, is covered in several general periodical databases (full text is available from 1980 in *LexisNexis Academic*, *Factiva*, and *ProQuest Newsstand*, among others).

Several newspaper-specific databases are available; your library may subscribe to one of the following (or have access through a consortium):

Gale's *National Newspaper Index* indexes several key U.S. newspapers. The *Christian Science Monitor, New York Times, Wall Street Journal* and *Washington Post* are covered from 1980; the *Los Angeles Times* is covered from 1982. This source can be an efficient and convenient way to find citations on various topics, which can then be followed up on in other databases or microfilm holdings (full text of these papers is not included).

Newspaper Source from EBSCO provides full-text coverage for nearly 400 newspapers, ranging from major dailies (*Chicago Tribune, Philadelphia Inquirer*) to regional papers (*Tulsa World, Grand Forks Herald*) to international publications (*Kuwait Times, Slovak Spectator*). More than 90 percent of the titles are provided in "selective" form, meaning that not all of the articles can be found in the database. Coverage for many titles goes back to 1997, although some begin much later. Also featured in this database are full-text transcripts of radio and television news programming from major media outlets, dating mostly from the mid-2000s.

ProQuest Newsstand provides more than 500 newspapers, mainly from the United States. There is no one *Newsstand* collection; instead, libraries subscribe to one or more packages containing publications from a particular state or region, or they can customize their own package. Approximately 70 percent of the newspapers are available in full-text. Coverage is from 1980 for some titles.

LexisNexis Academic carries the full text of more than 350 newspapers from the United States and abroad. Coverage for some (e.g., *The Washington Post*) goes back to the late 1970s. LexisNexis users can easily filter their searches to include only news sources by using the Quick or Guided News Search pages.

Finally, a good free "one-stop shopping" source to search for older newspaper articles is Google's News Archive Search (http://news.google.com/archivesearch), which searches for stories on people and events in older newspapers and generates an accompanying timeline. As with the newspaper Web sites described previously, some of the content is free, whereas other articles are available for a fee.

SPECIALIZED INDEXES

In addition to newspaper indexes, there are many other specialized types of indexes and databases. Some indexes are targeted at specific **age groups:** elementary school students, middle schoolers, or the high school bracket.

EBSCO *Primary Search* is a full-text database featuring more than 60 age-appropriate periodicals (e.g., *Cricket, Jack & Jill*) together with a number of biographies, images, maps, and encyclopedias. Records include a reading level indicator. *Middle Search Plus* is a similar database aimed at middle school-age children that covers more than 170 periodicals (of which more than 80% are full-text), along with reference works and a collection of primary source materials for U.S. history.

Infotrac Kids from Gale is aimed at the K-12 age group, and has almost 120 periodicals, all but 5 of which are full-text, as well as reference works (including *The Columbia Encyclopedia*) and selected articles from newspapers. *InfoTrac Junior Edition* overlaps with *Kids* while adding a great deal of content aimed at middle school students. It indexes more than 215 periodicals, more than 90 percent of them full-text, along with a smattering of reference sources, images, more than 300 full-color maps, and newspaper content. These databases offer a simple, icon-heavy interface designed to help children get started in their searching, as well as pointers on paper-writing.

Gale's *Student Resource Center* brings together more than 1,100 full-text periodicals and a bevy of primary source materials and reference works. Students can explore topics using a tabbed interface that categorizes relevant records from reference works, magazines, academic journals, news sources, creative works, primary sources, and multimedia content. The database even offers study guide questions. Subscription offerings range (Olympics-style) from a bare-bones "Bronze" to the more comprehensive "Gold." A "Junior Edition" aimed at middle school students is also available.

Other indexes cover particular types of **genres,** such as plays or short stories. The following indexes are provided by H. W. Wilson:

Short Story Index provides records for more than 96,000 stories from book and periodical sources, with coverage beginning in 1984. In addition to the usual access points—author, title, subject, date, and so on—users can search by theme, genre, narrative technique, or device. Such searches can be useful for both pleasure reading and school projects. The database itself does not have full-text stories, but it integrates with the library's OPAC and in some cases with other databases, allowing users to quickly find out if the story can be easily located on site or electronically.

Play Index is a similar database for dramatic works. It contains citations for more than 31,000 plays and 600 monologues, many of them published in collections that might not turn up in OPAC searching; coverage goes back to 1949. Users can search not only by subject, style, and genre, but also by size of cast, gender of characters, and intended age group. Records include information on staging requirements, making the index useful to drama classes and theater groups.

By searching *Biography Index,* users can find citations to biographical information ranging from antiquity to modern times, and in a number of formats, including books, periodicals, obituaries, interviews, and reviews. More than 3,000 periodicals and 2,000 books are covered, beginning in 1984.

Finally, some indexes focus on articles published in specific **subject areas** such as business, psychology, education, or history. Among those that may be useful for the general public are the following:

The *Education Resource Information Center (ERIC),* which is freely available from the U.S. Department of Education, indexes more than 650 education-related journals, with coverage of some going as far back as 1966. In some cases full text is provided, either by ERIC or by the publisher.

PubMed is a database of citations to medical literature maintained and provided for free by the U.S. National Library of Medicine. Its largest component is MEDLINE, which indexes more than 5,000 international (although primarily English-language) biomedical journals going as far back as the mid-1950s, along with some additional content. In some cases, *PubMed* citations link to full-text articles, which may be free or fee-based. This index can be accessed through a variety of front-ends on the Web.

H. W. Wilson provides a number of subject-based indexes, with a healthy dose of full-text content. Citations typically include abstracts and in many cases link out to the library's OPAC, other databases, and Web sites. Subject-specific titles include:

- *Education Full Text*
- *General Science Full Text*
- *Humanities Full Text*
- *Social Sciences Full Text*
- *Wilson Business Full Text*

These and more are included in Wilson's *OmniFile Full Text* database, which covers more than 4,000 journals, nearly 60 percent of them full-text (a "Select Edition" carries full-text records only).

The American Psychological Association's (APA) *PsycInfo* indexes more than 2,100 journals, along with books, book chapters, and dissertations. Some citations date back to the nineteenth century, and coverage is international in scope. *PsycInfo* is available directly from the APA or from a variety of vendors including EBSCO, OCLC FirstSearch, and ProQuest.

Gale's *LegalTrac* indexes 1,300 legal publications (law reviews, bar association journals, etc.), with more than 100 given in full text. Citations for some publications go back to 1980, and law-related articles from general-interest publications are also covered.

A recent trend has been for some database vendors, notably Gale, to provide databases that include *more* than just articles, clustered around a subject theme. So for instance, when you are helping a patron look for literary analysis of the works of Jane Smiley, and you search under her name (or her name and a particular work) in the *Literature Resource Center,* you find not only journal articles providing analysis and reviews, but also biographical information about the author, links to selected Web sites, access to entries in an encyclopedia of literature, a literary-historical timeline, and so forth.

From Literature Resource Center by Gale. Reprinted with permission of Gale, a division of Thomson Learning: www.thomsonrights.com. Fax 800-730-2215.

A few examples of these kinds of "information centers" are described next.

Gale's *Literature Resource Center* (LRC) displays search results from more than 300 full-text literary journals, reference works such as *Contemporary Authors,* relevant Web links, and a timeline linking the author's life and works to larger world events.

The *MLA Bibliography,* with citations for literary and humanities publications reaching back to the 1920s, can be added to the LRC as an optional module.

Searching for particular ailments in Gale's *Health & Wellness Resource Center* brings up an easily navigable display offering entries in reference works such as the *Gale Encyclopedia of Medicine,* citations to magazine and journal articles (from a selection of nearly 900 periodicals, most of them full-text), information on associated pharmaceuticals, pamphlets from health care organizations, and other resources.

Gale's *Business & Company Resource Center* presents information on companies using a tabbed display, providing reports from the business and popular press, a historical sketch, investment reports, financial tables, and other relevant resources. When applicable, users can easily navigate to an entity's parent company or subsidiaries.

Users of EBSCO's *Business Source Premier* can filter their search results to show articles from academic journals and popular magazines (more than 2,300 provided full-text), as well as company reports, industry profiles, and so on.

Aimed at school-age children, ProQuest's *SIRS Knowledge Source* responds to search queries on contemporary issues with a multitude of resources: full-text articles and essays, government documents, maps, and reference works. ProQuest also offers a monthly newsletter with ideas for integrating *Knowledge Source* into the school curriculum.

TRACKING DOWN SPECIFIC ARTICLES

During the past two decades, the number of periodicals and indexes available to most libraries has grown significantly. There are so many databases to choose from that it can sometimes be confusing. How do we know which ones cover which journals? How do we know if an article our patron is looking for is available full-text in one of the databases we have access to?

Fortunately there are tools to help us find out which journal titles are included in which indexes. Your library (or library consortium) may subscribe to one of the following:

Serials Solutions (http://www.serialssolutions.com) works from a customized list of databases provided by your library. When you enter a periodical title, it will tell you which of the databases contains full-text articles from that magazine or journal (and for what years); you can click on the database link to enter the database. You can also subscribe to its "article linker" feature, which allows you to provide more information about an article you are looking for, and in some cases, go straight to the article in the database. They also produce MARC Records for your online catalog, so that if you are searching for a magazine or journal title in your catalog, you will see (listed alongside your print holdings) which of your databases may contain electronic versions of the publication.

EBSCO A to Z (http://www.ebsco.com/atoz/) offers a similar service to libraries. Again, you can customize your list of databases so that patrons searching the A to Z product will find which of your databases cover which journals. As with *Serials Solutions,* you can choose to include your print journal titles in the list (so that patrons will know which titles may be available only in print).

Finally, *Ulrich's Periodicals Directory* (available in both printed volumes and online at ulrichsweb.com) offers a comprehensive listing of information about all kinds of "magazines, journals, newspapers, newsletters, 'zines and more," over a quarter of a million titles in all, from more than 200 countries. The records for these publications include pricing and publisher information, as well as where they are indexed. Libraries can also set up the capability to link from journal titles to full text (through Serials Solutions and several other databases) or to the record for a periodical in the library's catalog.

IN SUM

In today's world, so many libraries now belong to state or regional consortia, human networks that enable us to band together and to make better use of all the resources available to us over the computer networks. State- and regional-level virtual library projects have given even smaller library systems access to an impressive number of periodical indexes and databases. We have moved from having the *Reader's Guide,* and maybe another print index or two, to providing our patrons with multiple full-text periodical databases, including many free ones.

Don't be overwhelmed by the number of databases available to you, or by the fact that each may seem to have a slightly different look or feel. Try not to feel intimidated by the older print indexes your library may have either. Instead, take the time to gradually familiarize yourself with the periodical indexes and databases available, noticing which ones your patrons seem to prefer, observing how they differ from one another in look and feel, and practicing the basic search techniques covered in Chapter 4. You'll be an expert searcher in no time!

REVIEW

1. A high school student needs to find articles about Joseph McCarthy published while he was still in the Senate (in the 1950s). Which indexes might be of help?
2. Does your library currently provide online access to the *New York Times, Washington Post, Wall Street Journal,* or *Christian Science Monitor* through any of its databases?
3. Are your local newspapers and prominent regional dailies available for free on the Web? If so, how far back does coverage go, and is it complete or partial? If not, are they included in any databases your library subscribes to?

4.   Does your library include links to free indexes such as *PubMed* and *ERIC* on its Web site?

5.   Can patrons at your library easily learn whether a particular journal is available from your library electronically?

6.   What databases does your library provide that are useful for elementary schoolchildren? How about middle schoolers?

NOTES

1.   Napoleon Bonaparte, quoted in McLuhan, M. *Understanding media: The extensions of man.* London & New York: Routledge, 1964, 2001. p. 14.

2.   Roncevic, M. (2005). The e-ref invasion. *Library Journal, 130* (19), 8–10, 13.

3.   Current title lists of the periodicals included are available in each database, as well as at the publishers' Web sites.

CHAPTER 7

Finding Background Information and Definitions: Encyclopedias and Dictionaries

Both the man of the people and the scientist will always have equally as much to desire and instruction to find in an encyclopedia.[1]

ENCYCLOPEDIAS

An encyclopedia is defined in the *Oxford English Dictionary* as "the circle of learning," and, less poetically, as "a literary work containing extensive information on all branches of knowledge, usually arranged in alphabetical order."[2]

The encyclopedia has typically been the place we have gone in search of authoritative answers to our everyday questions: who Robespierre was, what chipmunks eat, when Queen Elizabeth I ruled England, where Fiji is located, why winter days are shorter than summer days. The encyclopedia of my childhood (and most likely, yours) was an impressive multivolume work, filled with such information, and waiting to bestow its knowledge upon us. It was a dominating presence in every library, as well as in many homes. (Rumor had it that Sam H, the smartest boy in our fifth-grade class, was reading the *Encyclopaedia Britannica* he had at home all the way through, and that he was already up to the Js!)

When you went to the *Encyclopaedia Britannica,* or the *Americana,* or the *World Book,* and turned to the Cs to find information on Chipmunks, or F for Fiji, a nugget of wisdom awaited you, a brief article on your topic, written by someone who was an expert and sometimes followed by a brief bibliography. It might be that your topic wasn't quite where you thought it would be; and then you might have to turn to the index volume where you would find (for instance) that Robespierre was discussed in a certain article on the French Revolution.

Print encyclopedias are still issued today, although sales of this format are certainly dwindling. Most of them still follow this basic layout, with alphabetically arranged entries supplemented by an index (although *Britannica* is somewhat more complicated). Just like library catalogs and periodical indexes before them, however, the major encyclopedias have all gone digital and are now available over the Web (and generally in CD-ROM and/or DVD as well). Alongside the traditional powerhouses (*Encyclopaedia Britannica, Encyclopedia Americana, Academic American Encyclopedia, World Book, Compton's*), a couple of electronic newcomers have emerged, notably, Microsoft's *Encarta* and, in recent years, *Wikipedia,* a freely available, grassroots project that has challenged the very idea of what an encyclopedia is.

Of course, the digital versions of encyclopedias have great advantages: they are searchable by keyword; you can link immediately to related topics of interest; they can be kept updated with the latest information; and wonderful multimedia files are often available to illustrate concepts. *Britannica*'s entry for "The Heart," for instance, includes animated videos demonstrating the circulatory system and the heart's various functions, as well as video of an actual human heart beating.[3] In some cases, the readers themselves are able to suggest additions or changes to the text in the encyclopedia.

Whether in print or electronic format, the encyclopedia remains a valuable starting point for research on a wide range of topics—a place where you can quickly gain a basic understanding of a subject and often learn where to look for more information. When considering the usefulness of an encyclopedia, it is especially important to be aware of how in-depth its treatment of a given topic is (and whether it offers suggestions for "further reading"); how current it is; and what age group it is intended for (an encyclopedia article that you understand perfectly may be incomprehensible to an eight-year-old!).

The following sections describe major encyclopedias currently available in libraries.

For Adults

Encyclopaedia Britannica is the quintessential encyclopedia. First published in 1768, it continues to be available in print: the latest 32-volume edition, which appeared in 2005, featured more than 65,000 articles and 24,000 illustrations. The contents of the encyclopedia are also available in CD-ROM and DVD format, and now the print edition is generally sold as a "suite," together with other print and electronic resources (including a year's access to *Britannica Online*).

Britannica Online (http://www.britannica.com), the Internet version of the *Encylopaedia,* made its first appearance in 1994. It includes the full text of the articles contained in the print Britannica, plus many additional features: videos, timelines, access to Merriam-Webster's dictionaries and thesauri, links to more than 300,000 magazine and journal articles (as well as to selected Web sites), and news headlines. Basic and advanced search options are provided, as well as an index and an "A-Z browsing" list of entries. Britannica products are offered to libraries in various subscription packages; the public library package, for instance, includes access to the content of *Encyclopaedia Britannica, Britannica Elementary Encyclopedia,* and *Compton's Encyclopedia* (a lavishly illustrated encyclopedia aimed at 10- to 17-year-olds), along with many of the "extras" enumerated previously. Free access to a much abbreviated version (*Britannica Concise Encyclopedia*) is available without a subscription at their Web site.

Britannica's strengths lie in the scope of its coverage and the level of its writing; many experts have contributed to it over the years, and it remains impressively authoritative. A box for suggesting changes to content has recently been added, reflecting a growing understanding of the ways in which public participation can add value to an encyclopedia.

Encyclopedia Americana emerged more than 175 years ago as the worthy American rival to *Britannica.* The most recent print edition of this well-regarded encyclopedia was issued in 2006 by Scholastic. Its 30 volumes feature more than 45,000 articles (alphabetically arranged), numerous maps and illustrations, and an index.

A Web-based version of *Americana* is offered through Grolier Online (at http://go.grolier.com). An eye-catching Web site invites readers to search the encyclopedia (both basic and advanced search options are available), to browse by subject area, to peruse biographical profiles, or to search a current events and news database. The online version of *Americana* includes access to several American Heritage dictionaries, as well as the Roget's II *New Thesaurus.*

Microsoft's *Encarta* (http://encarta.msn.com) is a widely used digital encyclopedia, which many of your patrons may be familiar with. Originally based on the contents of Funk & Wagnall's and later Collier's encyclopedias,[4] *MSN Encarta* has evolved greatly since 1993, when it first hit the market as a CD-ROM encyclopedia. *Encarta Premium's* 60,000 + articles, and 25,000 image/multimedia files are currently available on the Web by subscription; a DVD version is also available for purchase. The encyclopedia is readily searchable and includes an interactive atlas and access to a Homework Center developed to help students. A small subset of 4,500 articles, as well as a dictionary, thesaurus, and atlas, are available for free at the *Encarta* Web site.

Wikipedia (http://www.wikipedia.org) was established by Jimmy Wales in 2001 as a free Web-based encyclopedia that is collaboratively written and open to editing by anyone with an Internet connection. A favorite source of general information for many Web-surfers, its strengths include the provision of up-to-date information on a tremendous range of topics: as of early 2008, it boasted more than 9 million articles (2.2 million of them in English) written by 75,000 active contributors. *Wikipedia* is available in 10 major languages; it is extensively hyperlinked, easily searchable (and browsable), and articles from the site can also be retrieved through major search engines such as Google or Yahoo.

Of course, there are disadvantages to having such an open source; as stated in *Wikipedia* itself, "articles and subject areas sometimes suffer from significant omissions, and while misinformation and vandalism are usually corrected quickly, this does not always happen."[5] The writing style and level also vary greatly. On the other hand, a 2005 study published in *Nature* found that *Wikipedia* "comes close to *Britannica* in terms of the accuracy of its science entries"; reviewers of 42 articles appearing in each of the publications found 4 serious errors and 162 minor problems in *Wikipedia* entries, compared to 4 serious errors and 123 minor problems in *Britannica* entries.[6] (*Encyclopedia Britannica* has refuted the findings.)[7]

Despite its shortcomings, *Wikipedia* does provide a useful starting point for information on some topics, at no cost. Patrons using this source, however, should be made fully aware of its "grassroots" nature and the problems that this can sometimes create.

For Young Adults and Children

Perhaps the best known encyclopedia produced specifically for children is the *World Book Encyclopedia,* written for elementary through high school students. *World Book* has been in publication since 1917. The 2007 edition features 24 volumes of articles carefully composed by 3,800 contributors, with more than 27,000 illustrations.

An online version has been available since 1998; like many of the other online encyclopedias, free "snippets" of articles may be accessed at http://www.worldbook. com/wb/Browse?id=ency. A subscription to *World Book Online* provides access to more than 25,000 articles from the encyclopedia, as well as numerous videos, animations, and sounds, and to *World Book Kids,* an online resource for younger students based on the *Student Discovery Encyclopedia.* An atlas, dictionary, and student activity center are also available at the Web site.

Britannica and Grolier also produce encyclopedias for children and teenagers. Britannica publishes *Compton's Encyclopedia* (both online and in print) for the middle and high school set, as well as the *Britannica Elementary Encyclopedia* (available online) for younger students. Grolier publishes the *Grolier Multimedia Encyclopedia* (online only) for middle and high school students; *The New Book of Knowledge* (available online and in print) is written for elementary schoolchildren.

In the case of each of these resources, more information and free trials for libraries are available at their Web sites (with the exception of *Wikipedia,* which does not require a subscription). In considering which of these encyclopedias and in which format(s) are right for your patrons, it's a good idea to carefully explore the Britannica,

Grolier, Encarta, and World Book Web sites, assessing the various "packages" of products they may make available and evaluating their encyclopedias according to the criteria in Chapter 3. Also consider which encyclopedias your library has traditionally collected (and why) and talk with your patrons about their preferences: they will ultimately be the people who use (or do not use) the encyclopedias your library provides.

Concise Encyclopedias

In addition to the more comprehensive encyclopedias, there are also some useful compact encyclopedias on the market. In printed form, they usually comprise only one volume, which contains brief information about a range of subjects, alphabetically arranged. This type of content is now widely available on the Web, for free. For instance, the *Columbia Encyclopedia,* which has been issued since the 1920s (and is now in its sixth edition), can still be purchased in printed form; its 50,000 entries can also be freely consulted at http://www.infoplease.com/encyclopedia/.

And, as mentioned previously, brief information on "people, places and things" is freely available for nonsubscribers at the *Britannica, Encarta,* and *World Book* Web sites (at http://concise.britannica.com/, http://encarta.msn.com/, and http://www.worldbook.com/wb/Browse?id=ency). Of course, the Web sites always encourage visitors to subscribe to the encyclopedias to gain access to fuller articles!

Subject Encyclopedias

Finally, subject-specific encyclopedias on various topics abound. These kinds of encyclopedias offer general information on specific subjects such as areas of knowledge (e.g., Wiley's *Encyclopedia of Physics*), animals (e.g., Elsevier's *Encyclopedia of Insects*), diseases (e.g., the *Gale Encyclopedia of Cancer*), places (e.g., the *Encyclopedia of Chicago* from the University of Chicago Press), events (e.g., Gale's *Encyclopedia of the Great Depression*), or time periods (e.g., *Encyclopedia of the Victorian Era* from Grolier).

The usefulness of such sources in a small library setting should be carefully assessed. As with any source, when deciding which subject-specific encyclopedias to purchase, you should consider the needs of the customers of your library. Are your health-related resources heavily used? Consider buying the *Gale Encyclopedia of Medicine* for your collection. Is there a strong musical or artistic community in your area? Perhaps the *Encyclopedia of American Folk Art* would be a reasonable purchase. Geography matters as well: if you live in Tennessee, the *Encyclopedia of Appalachia* might be a good book to acquire; if you're in Iowa, the *Encyclopedia of Iowa* might be more fitting.

Subject-specific encyclopedias are sometimes included in the collections of resources offered by publishers. If your library belongs to a consortium that subscribes to the Gale Virtual Reference Library or to some of the sources in NetLibrary's Reference Center, for instance, you may have access to an impressive number of specialized online encyclopedias.

DICTIONARIES AND THESAURI

Dictionaries make the meanings of words clear to us. They are also helpful for clarifying questions about spelling, pronunciation disputes, and word origins. A dictionary of the English language is a standard reference tool found in every library, most classrooms, and many homes in the United States. If you close your eyes, perhaps you can still picture yourself as a child, asking how to spell a word or what it meant, only to hear your parent or teacher urge you to "*Look it up!*"

In addition to English-language dictionaries, there are many other kinds of dictionaries we may not think about using everyday: dictionaries of languages other than English, bilingual (or multilingual) dictionaries that provide us with translations, etymological dictionaries showing word origins, dictionaries of slang, rhyming dictionaries, "visual" dictionaries, and subject-specific dictionaries that explain the terminology of a particular topic or field. There are also dictionaries of synonyms and antonyms, and thesauri, which help us with word selection. This section focuses on English-language dictionaries and thesauri; some of the better known publishers of bilingual dictionaries are mentioned as well.

The *Oxford English Dictionary*

The "mother of all dictionaries" is the *Oxford English Dictionary (OED),* an impressive attempt to catalog the language. The *OED,* as it is familiarly known, includes more than half a million words from past and present-day English; along with pronunciation and definitions, it gives word histories and illustrates the evolution of their meanings through the use of quotations. The entry for "liberal," for instance, traces in painstaking detail the evolution of each of the word's six meanings (three of which are subdivided). The first of these shows that it was originally used (the first examples given are from the fourteenth century) as "the distinctive epithet of those 'arts' or 'sciences' that were considered 'worthy of a free man'"—and demonstrates through a sequence of quotations how this meaning is preserved today in the term "liberal arts." Such entries, in addition to being great fodder for cocktail party talk, are of particular interest to students and scholars studying older texts.

The *OED* runs to 20 volumes in its printed form; it is also available through a Web-based subscription (which is frequently updated), and on CD-ROM. The cost of subscription may be prohibitive to smaller libraries,[8] but rates for consortia are available, or you may want to consider whether it is feasible to purchase the CD-ROM version of this unique resource (currently priced at $295.00) for your library.

Unabridged Dictionaries

Like the *OED,* unabridged dictionaries represent an attempt to provide a comprehensive listing of words in a language, along with their pronunciations, meanings, and (to some extent) etymologies. When your patrons come to you with a highly unusual word, needing a definition or confirmation of the correct spelling (and they will), it is *essential* to have access to an unabridged dictionary in your library.

Currently, the two main unabridged dictionaries available in English are *Webster's Third New International Dictionary* (with more than 470,000 entries) and the *Random House Webster's Unabridged Dictionary* (with 315,000 entries). The "core" of *Webster's Unabridged* dates to 1961, but the most recent edition updates this to 2002; it is available in print, as an online subscription (see http://www.merriam-websterunabridged. com), on CD-ROM, and as a downloadable e-book. The *Random House Webster's Unabridged* has been updated to 2001 and is available in print and on CD-ROM; a portion of the dictionary is available for free as the Infoplease dictionary (see http://www.info please.com/dictionary.html).

Abridged Dictionaries

An unabridged dictionary is a wonderful resource, but a less comprehensive dictionary will probably be appropriate for most word-related reference questions. You will probably want to have several copies of abridged (or "desk") dictionaries in your library. *Merriam-Webster's Collegiate Dictionary* (11th edition), with 225,000 definitions, is available in print, on CD-ROM, and by subscription at http://www.merriam-webstercollegiate.com. An extensive subset of the dictionary is freely available at http://www.m-w.com/. *The American Heritage Dictionary*, 4th edition (2000), is also a worthy choice. With more than 90,000 entries and many illustrations, it is a solid work, available in print and freely available online at http://www.bartleby.com/61/. Incidentally, in addition to the standard definitions, pronunciation, and etymology, the online versions of each of these dictionaries have sound files that allow us to hear a word being pronounced—a very handy feature!

Dictionaries for Children

The definitions given in adult dictionaries may be difficult for children to understand. Fortunately, several excellent dictionaries are made just for kids. Thorndike-Barnhart, which has published dictionaries for children for many years, offers a selection of books for different age groups, including a *Children's Dictionary* for elementary school, a *Junior Dictionary* for middle schoolers, and a *Student Dictionary* for slightly older children. The *World Book Dictionary,* available as part of many of their subscription packages, is based on their Thorndike-Barnhart product. The *Macmillan Dictionary for Children* (4th revised edition, 2001) is an attractive, clearly laid out dictionary for children in the elementary grades; a *Dictionary for Students* is also available. Merriam-Webster offers a free online dictionary just for children at http://wordcentral.com, as well as some fun word games and an open dictionary where people of all ages can submit their own entries for new words.

It should be evident from the preceding descriptions, that a number of reputable dictionaries make at least a portion of their content freely available online. Other on-line sites, such as the frequently used dictionary.com or onelook.com, draw on some of these resources; see the list of sources at http://dictionary.reference.com/help/about. html, or the sources cited when you look up a word in onelook.com. (For example, for the word *terrorism*, onelook.com gives the searcher links to more than 20 different on-line entries, including those from the *Encarta World English Dictionary, Merriam-Webster 10th ed., The Cambridge Dictionary of American English, Webster's Revised Abridged* (1913 edition), *The New Dictionary of Cultural Literacy,* and *Wikipedia*). When we or our patrons use online sites such as these, it is important to be aware of the source (or sources) of the definitions we are viewing and to carefully consider where these definitions are coming from.

As well as having a selection of English-language dictionaries in your library, you will probably also want to select some authoritative bilingual dictionaries for your reference collection. Which dictionaries you decide to collect will depend on the languages spoken in your community and taught in schools, community colleges, and universities in the area. HarperCollins, Oxford, Larousse, and Cassell are among the most recognized and respected publishers of bilingual dictionaries. On the Internet, foreignword. com taps into more than 265 freely available online dictionaries to offer translations in more than 70 languages (as well as text translations of many of these languages); http:// www.word2word.com/ is another useful free site for languages.

Thesauri

A thesaurus is an indispensable tool for students and writers. In this day and age of word processing, many of us have become accustomed to using the thesaurus built into Microsoft Word. There are other options; be sure to have at least a couple available in your library. In print, *Roget's International Thesaurus* features "more than 330,000 words and phrases organized into 1,075 categories"[9] with a comprehensive index to all words. Roget's also offers a *College Thesaurus* in dictionary form for those who prefer a straightforward A to Z arrangement. Oxford, American Heritage, and Merriam-Webster all offer thesauri based on their vast databases of definitions; Merriam-Webster's is available online, at http://www.m-w.com/.

IN SUM

Encyclopedias and dictionaries remain a crucial resource to any library. Patrons will use them to find background information, check simple facts, look up definitions, and for more sophisticated research on narrower topics or on the history of the language. When selecting encyclopedias, both print and electronic, be aware of your particular users' needs: Which populations might use subject-specific encyclopedias? Which age groups do you need to serve? Knowing about the full range of encyclopedias, including free Web-based versions, will help you serve a wide variety of patrons. Likewise, appreciating the differences between various types of dictionaries (historical, unabridged, abridged, children's, bilingual, and thesauri) will help you direct your patrons to essential aids to reading and writing.

REVIEW

1. Look in three or four print and online encyclopedias that are available to you for information on a topic about which you are well informed (for instance: "whale," "bullfighting," "poverty"). How comprehensive is the coverage? What level of reader does each address? How are links and multimedia content used in the online versions?

2. Take a look at *Wikipedia*'s "Talk" page for the topic you looked up (e.g., http://en.wikipedia.org/wiki/Talk:Poverty). What does a page like this tell you about the resource, both positive and negative? How might it affect your willingness to recommend it to a patron?

3. What makes the *OED* special? Given its cost, does your library need it?

4. What is the difference between an abridged and unabridged dictionary?

5. Choose a word (for instance: hallow (noun), organic, conundrum) and look it up in dictionaries of various types (abridged, unabridged, *OED,* etc.), as well as in dictionary.com or onelook.com. Which of these resources would you recommend to a patron seeking quick definitions of unfamiliar words? To a patron reading an eighteenth-century text? What will you do if a patron says he or she has already looked in a dictionary and has not found the meaning?

NOTES

1. Diderot. *Encyclopédie* (translator: Philip Stewart). Available online at http://hdl.handle.net/2027/spo.did2222.0000.004.

2. *Oxford English Dictionary*. (2007). Oxford, England: Oxford University Press. Available online at http://www.oed.com

3. *Encyclopædia Britannica Online*, s.v. "Heart," http://search.eb.com.libaccess.sjlibrary.org/eb/article-9039718example (accessed April 13, 2007).

4. Books & other things (1993). *Book Report, 11* (4), 41–44; Jasco, P. (1999). 1999 editions of general-interest encyclopedias. *Computers in Libraries, 19* (6), 30–32.

5. Wikipedia: About, 2008. Available online at http://en.wikipedia.org/wiki/Wikipedia:About

6.   Giles, J. (2005, 2006). Internet encyclopaedias go head to head. *Nature*. Available online at http://www.nature.com/nature/journal/v438/n7070/full/438900a.html

7.   Encyclopaedia Britannica, Inc. (2006). Fatally flawed: Refuting the recent study on encyclopedic accuracy by the journal *Nature*. Available online at http://corporate.britannica. com/britannica_nature_response.pdf

8.   See pricing at http://oed.com/subscribe/

9.   From the book cover.

CHAPTER 8

Finding Facts Fast: Ready Reference

You will excuse me, dear Readers, that I afford you no Eclipses of the Moon this Year. The Truth is, I do not find they do you any Good. When there is one you are apt in observing it to expose yourselves too much and too long to the Night Air, whereby great Numbers of you catch Cold. Which was the Case last Year, to my very great Concern. However, if you will promise to take more Care of your selves, you shall have a fine one to stare at, the Year after next.[1]

If you venture into an unknown library and head toward the public service desk, you are likely to see that the librarians have a shelf or two of titles that they want to keep close at hand. Ask to see the computer at the desk; the librarians will probably have bookmarked the online versions of some of these sources as well (along with a few other choice sites).

These are the "ready reference" sources, sources that are so handy for answering questions that no librarian would want to be without them. If a fire breaks out in the library, these will be books librarians grab as they run out the door, assuming all patrons and staff are safe, of course! If shipwrecked on a desert island, these will be the sources librarians hope will wash ashore because they will provide them with valuable knowledge and hours of entertainment.

83

Ready reference sources are the sources that are packed with handy facts, the kinds of facts that people often ask about. If a patron has a "quick question" about a date, a phone number, a famous quotation, a country, or a statistic, you can turn to a ready reference source with assurance that it is likely to have the desired information. A good ready reference source is up-to-date, accurate, and well indexed. Although they are full of facts, such sources often make for surprisingly good reading—especially for a curious reference librarian!

What follows are my **"lucky seven,"** the seven ready reference sources I would take with me (in that shipwreck or trial-by-fire situation). Each source is representative of a broader category of sources that will be described as well. These sources are chosen on the basis of their authority and proven usefulness in reference work, but there are many other valuable sources in each category, some of which are also described.

ALMANACS

Almanacs are handy collections of fascinating facts about a wide variety of people, places, and things. The ***World Almanac and Book of Facts*** is an excellent example of this type of reference source. First published in 1868, it has been going strong ever since. Each annual edition features a "year in review" section, with highlights from the preceding year followed by sections on economics, crime, famous personalities, science and technology, consumer information, U.S. politics and population, world history and culture, and sports. All of this is followed by an index to lead readers quickly to the trivia of their choice. Want to browse through a list of famous artists, photographers, and sculptors and then turn to a summary of the basic laws of physics, and then check out the 100 most populous cities in the United States, read up on the Republic of Tajikstan, and quiz your friend as to who won the Super Bowl in 1974? Then this is certainly the source for you! The *World Almanac* is also available online, on CD-ROM, and in a format that can be downloaded to a PDA (personal digital assistant)—all for a subscription price.

The *Time Almanac* (formerly known as the *Information Please Almanac*) is another worthy example of this type of source. Like the *World Almanac,* it is packed with a smorgasbord of information. Its index is right up front (an unusual move) followed by an abundance of information on elections, animals, holidays, the Olympics, state and country profiles, prizes, and much more. The *Time Almanac* is also freely available on the Web, at http://www.infoplease.com.

DIRECTORIES

Directories are another useful type of source for locating quick factual information, in this case, information for locating individuals or organizations. A good example of a directory, and possibly the first reference book you ever encountered, is the **local phone book.** This resource commonly lists individuals and businesses by name, giving their phone numbers and addresses as well. A "yellow pages" section lists businesses by category (and includes the same contact information of phone number and address).

Of course, the phone book, like so many other sources, has gone digital. Free online directories such as switchboard.com and anywho.com allow us to search locally and nationally for individuals and businesses by name, by category, and even by phone number.

Other types of directories to bear in mind as you build your reference collection are directories of companies (like *Standard & Poor's Directory*), associations (the *Encyclopedia of Associations*), colleges (*Peterson's 4-year Colleges*), and professionals (*Martindale-Hubbell Law Directory*). Many directories offer more than just contact information; for instance, they may offer profiles of people or institutions, or earnings information for companies. The major titles will offer both print and online versions (usually for a price). But the basic purpose, to provide organized, accessible information about individuals and/or organizations and group them together in useful ways, remains constant.

QUOTATION SOURCES

Quotation sources are wonderful tools to have at hand for the student who needs an opening statement for a speech, for the person who remembers a part of a quote and needs to complete it, for the librarian who has just been asked: "Who said 'o what a tangled web we weave, when first we practice to deceive'?"

Bartlett's Familiar Quotations is a much beloved reference tool, dating back to 1855. Its aim, as Mr. Bartlett wrote in the first edition, is "to show, to some extent, the obligations our language owes to various authors for numerous phrases and familiar quotations which have become 'household words.'"[2] Notable quotations are arranged in chronological order (by authors' birthdates); a source is provided for each quote. An author index appears at the front of the book, and a keyword index at the back leads the reader to the appropriate page and number of quotation on the page, for any given quote they are seeking. The 10th edition (from 1919) is freely available online, at http://bartleby.com/100.

Quotation sources are plentiful. Several others, in fact, are listed at bartleby.com, including *Simpson's Contemporary Quotations* (1988)*, Respectfully Quoted: A Dictionary of Quotations* (1989), and *The Columbia World of Quotations* (1996). There are also many other specialized quotations sources to choose from such as *African American Quotations, Quotations on the Vietnam War, Scholastic Treasury of Quotations for Children,* or the *Ultimate Dictionary of Sports Quotations*. The key is to choose your words (and your reference sources!) wisely.

HANDBOOKS, MANUALS, GUIDES

Handbooks, manuals, and guides provide useful information organized around a particular topic. They often have a "how to" theme to them as well. For instance, Chilton's automobile repair manuals tell us how to fix cars; the *Rough Guides* to Australia or China provide abundant information for travelers interested in exploring different parts of the world.

One shining example of the "handbook" genre is the ***Occupational Outlook Handbook,*** which is published every two years by the U.S. Department of Labor. This handbook offers a magnificent starting point for people interested in exploring different types of jobs whether they are schoolchildren, college students, adults seeking a career change, or people who are simply curious. More than 800 occupations are described in a fair amount of detail; working conditions, the number of jobs available, training required, the job outlook, and typical earnings are given for each one. At the end of every entry, related occupations and sources of additional information are listed. In the print version, occupations are grouped in clusters, with an alphabetical index of occupations at the end. This resource is also freely available online at http://www.bls.gov/oco/; the user-friendly Web site is browsable by occupation "cluster," as well as being searchable by keyword, and also includes an "A to Z" index.

Handbooks and manuals vary widely in their subject matter. A second interesting example, very different from the *Occupational Outlook Handbook,* is the *Merck Manual of Diagnosis and Therapy.* First published in 1899, this manual includes 23 sections covering different types of medical disorders, along with sections on obstetrics and gynecology, pediatrics, clinical pharmacology, and poisoning, all followed by a detailed index. Each medical condition includes information on symptoms and signs, diagnosis, and treatment. While written for health care practitioners, and therefore sometimes difficult to read, the authority of the *Merck Manual* is uncontested. (Consider consulting a resource like the American Medical Association's *Family Medical Guide* for information that is easier to understand.) The *Merck Manual* is also available for free online (at http://www.merck.com/mmpe/) and as a PDA download.

SOURCES OF COUNTRY INFORMATION

It is essential for every librarian to be able to provide timely, accurate information on countries and their leaders. A number of authoritative sources exist for this very purpose. Among the all-time favorites is the ***CIA World Factbook,*** issued annually by the U.S. government.

All of the world's countries are succinctly described in this source. Brief sections on history and geography are followed by up-to-date information on the population, government, economy, communication, transportation, the military, and any transnational disputes in which the country is involved. Flags and simple maps of the countries are included, and major international organizations are described in an appendix. The *World Factbook* is also freely available online at https://www.cia.gov/library/publications/the-world-factbook/.

Another longtime favorite resource in this category is the *Statesman's Yearbook,* issued annually since 1863. The first part of this book gives excellent coverage of international organizations, starting with the United Nations and including numerous other organizations. Part two is a listing of countries of the world. For each country, the publication includes a map, along with information on the country's history, population and social statistics, politics and government, industry, communications, social institutions, religion, and culture. Brief biographies of current leaders are also provided (and these can be fascinating). An online version of the *Yearbook* is available to subscribers at http://www.statesmansyearbook.com/.

CHRONOLOGIES

Calendars and chronologies are fun resources for the amateur historian to peruse. The time periods covered vary greatly from source to source, ranging from the beginning of history as we understand it, to particular eras, centuries, decades, or even just a single year in some sources.

The Timetables of History takes a broad look at recorded history; according to Daniel J. Boorstin (former librarian of Congress) it gives us "a feel for the fluidity and many sidedness of past experience."[3] Coverage in the fourth edition starts at 5000 B.C. and runs through 2004. For each era and beginning in the year A.D. 500, each year, it lists landmarks and notable events in seven categories, displayed side by side: history and politics; literature and theater; religion, philosophy, and learning; visual arts; music; science, technology, and growth; and daily life. Index entries refer the reader to a year and a column (A through G). So if we look up the year 1908, for example, we can find that H. H. Asquith was the British prime minister, Simone de Beauvoir was born, the first steel and glass building was constructed, ammonia was synthesized for the first time, and fountain pens became popular. Although it has been called Western-centric by some (it is based on a popular German work), this reference source is lots of fun, nonetheless.

An example of a more narrowly focused chronology is *Chase's Calendar of Events,* which approaches time in a very different way. Issued once a year, this source is arranged like a calendar, with each day showing an interesting sampling of events: national and international observances and holidays, festivals, religious observances, anniversaries, and birthdays. Looking in the 2007 volume, we can see that March 15, in addition to being the "Ides of March" and "True Confessions" Day, also marks the admission of Maine into the Union, and is Belarus's Constitution Day, the start of the NCAA-Division I Wrestling Championships, the model Fabio's birthday, and "Absolutely Incredible Kid" day. The calendar in *Chase's* is followed by lists of specially designated months, astronomical phenomena, presidential proclamations, annual awards, and a comprehensive index. A CD-ROM of the annual events is also included.

STATISTICAL SOURCES

Quick statistics on subjects are often requested in a library: How many people live in South Dakota? How long is the average lifespan in the United States? How much money does the average worker in my state earn? The answers to these questions, and many more, can be found in the *Statistical Abstract of the U.S.* Published annually since 1878, the *Statistical Abstract* includes social, political, and economic statistics gathered from government and private sources and displayed clearly in tables. Although the statistics are sometimes a few years old, sources are provided for each table (so the reader can easily find more information), and a brief International Statistics section is also included. A helpful index guides the user to information contained in each table.

The *Statistical Abstract* is also freely available online (all the way back to 1878) at http://www.census.gov/compendia/statab/. The online edition includes the index to tables and is also searchable by keyword; for more recent editions, many tables are available in excel format, and hyperlinks to the original sources of information are often provided.

As a "ready reference" source, the *Statistical Abstract* is truly without peers in the statistical world; however, the parent site where the online version resides (http://www.census.gov) deserves careful exploration by the serious librarian. Here you will find all kinds of statistical data on people and businesses. The *American FactFinder* tool is particularly useful for calling up statistical information, and the A to Z index of the Census Web site is also helpful. This site should continue to evolve and become ever more usable in the future.

IN SUM

Librarians have some concern that, as people become adept at searching the Internet, the number of ready reference questions is falling. Nowadays, the argument goes, anyone can Google "Albania" and pull up factual information on the country, or can quickly search for the source of a quotation. Although some types of questions may be easier to research than ever before, there is still a demand for ready reference service, even in a highly digital world.[4] It is important to be acquainted with some of the "classic" ready reference sources (many of which are now available in online format themselves) because of their proven worth in answering questions over the years and the high degree of authority associated with them. These are sources of known value to you as a reference librarian.

REVIEW

Match the questions with the most likely source of information for finding the answers:

1. When will Venus be visible this year? What were some of the major plane crashes over the last 70 years?
2. What percentage of voting-age Americans voted in 2004? How many people in the United States speak Tagalog at home?
3. What are some famous comments about music? Who said that "all happy families resemble one another"?
4. What are the employment prospects for postal workers? What is the median hourly rate for electricians?
5. What are the names of the active political parties in Pakistan? What percentage of South Africa's population is infected with HIV?
6. What are the names of and contact information for museums in Pittsburgh, PA? I jotted down a telephone number and can't remember what it's for; can I find out?
7. What were some important events that happened the year I was born?
8. What is Munchausen syndrome and how is it usually treated?

   a) *Bartlett's Familiar Quotations*
   b) *Timetables of History*
   c) *CIA World Factbook*
   d) *World Almanac and Book of Facts*
   e) *Switchboard.com*
   f) *Merck Manual*
   g) *Statistical Abstract of the U.S.*
   h) *Occupational Outlook Handbook*

NOTES

1. Franklin, B. (1976). *Poor Richard: The almanacks for the years 1733–1758.* New York: Paddington Press Ltd., 1738. p. 62.
2. Bartlett, J. & Kaplan, J. (1992). *Bartlett's familiar quotations: A collection of passages, phrases, and proverbs traced to their sources in ancient and modern literature* (16th ed.). Boston: Little, Brown. p. vii.
3. Grun, B. (2005). *The timetables of history* (4th ed.). New York: Touchstone. Foreword.
4. Radford, M.L. & Connaway, L.S. (2007, June). *Not dead yet! Ready reference in live chat reference.* Presented at the 13th RUSA New Reference Research Forum, American Library Association, Washington, DC.

CHAPTER 9

Using the Web to Reach Your Patrons and Help Them Find Information

Cybrarian (noun): a person whose job is to find, collect, and manage information that is available on the World Wide Web.[1]

In previous chapters, we discussed various types of resources for locating books, articles, background information, definitions, and factual information. I hope that you have become acquainted (or reacquainted) with some of the core library reference sources. A number of these sources, as we have seen, have a long history of publication going back for many years; others are more recent.

Regardless of their age, almost all of these core sources have been affected, in one way or another, by the public emergence and rapid growth of the Internet since the early 1990s. Established sources, such as the *Oxford English Dictionary* and the *Statistical Abstract of the United States,* have shifted shape and are now available in highly searchable, user-friendly Web-based formats (although the print editions of these titles still have their place). New sources (such as the *Internet Movie Database* or *Wikipedia*) have been "born digital," allowing for previously unimagined types of display and levels of user input. The Web offers reference librarians fresh (and ever-evolving) possibilities for providing excellent service to our patrons.

This chapter examines three specific ways to enhance reference services through intelligent use of the Web:

- Identifying and using free, high-quality Web sources
- Building your library's reference Web pages
- Offering e-mail and perhaps even chat or instant message reference service over the Web

FINDING AND USING THE "BEST" FREE WEB SOURCES

Previous chapters have described the need to be familiar with several major search engines and to feel comfortable using basic techniques for searching the Web (and evaluating the results of your searches). In addition to conducting searches, it is essential to be aware of some of the most important collections of freely available Web sources.

For decades, librarians have worked to assemble useful, usable reference collections. As sources migrated to the Web, we have begun to apply our talents here as well. As suggested in Chapter 3, it's a good idea to get acquainted with some of the major "portals" to free reference sources that are available on the Web, bearing in mind the needs of your community as you do. Several popular portals were mentioned in passing: the Internet Public Library reference section, the Librarians' Internet Index, and Refdesk.com. Brief descriptions of these three, plus four more high quality reference portals, follow.

1. ALA Best Free Reference Web Sites (1999–present)
   http://www.ala.org/ala/rusa/rusaourassoc/rusasections/mars/marspubs/
   MARSBESTIndex.htm

Each year since 1999, the Machine-Assisted Reference Section (MARS) of the American Library Association's Reference and User Services Association (RUSA) has produced an annotated list of approximately 30 excellent, free Web sites. An alphabetical index of all of the selected sites is available at the URL above—or you can look through the annotated lists for individual years at http://www.ala.org/ala/rusa/rusaouras soc/rusasections/mars/marspubs/publications.htm. Criteria for selection can be found on the MARS Web site and include "quality, depth, and usefulness of content;" usefulness for ready reference; accessibility; ease of use; currency; authority; and uniqueness.[2]

2. BUBL LINK Catalogue of Internet Sources: Reference
   http://bubl.ac.uk/link/r/reference.htm

The BUBL Information Service (sponsored by the University of Strathclyde's Centre for Digital Library Research in Glasgow, Scotland) has been in existence since 1990. It provides a subject listing of Internet resources of interest to researchers in the United Kingdom (and others as well), using the Dewey Decimal system. Each

Web site has been evaluated, annotated, and assigned a Dewey class number by staff at the University. Although potentially useful reference sources are scattered throughout BUBL, many core resources are pulled together at the URL listed here.

3.   Internet Public Library: Reference
      http://www.ipl.org/div/subject/browse/ref00.00.00

Founded in 1995 at the University of Michigan (and currently hosted by Drexel University's College of Information Science and Technology), the Internet Public Library (or IPL) seeks to serve Internet users by "finding, evaluating, selecting, organizing, describing, and creating information resources," as well as by providing direct assistance (by answering e-mail reference questions).[3] Their extensive lists of carefully selected, categorized, annotated Web sites include numerous reference-type sources (defined by the IPL as "basic research tools such as almanacs, dictionaries and encyclopedias"),[4] available at the preceding URL.

4.   Librarians' Internet Index: Ready Reference and Quick Facts
      http://search.lii.org/index.jsp?more=SubTopic10

Librarians' Internet Index (LII) has been in existence in one form or another since the early 1990s. It aims "to provide a well-organized point of access for reliable, trustworthy, librarian-selected websites."[5] Only freely available information is included in the LII; librarians closely examine each site's content, authority, scope and audience, design, functionality, and "shelf life" as well. The handy "Ready Reference" section includes numerous dictionaries, encyclopedias, statistical sources, phone books, calendars, and much more. There are multiple ways to search for resources on the site, and you can sign up to receive a newsletter every week that lists the latest additions to LII.

5.   Library of Congress Virtual Reference Shelf
      http://www.loc.gov/rr/askalib/virtualref.html

This is a succinct, no-nonsense listing of some of the online reference sources deemed most valuable by reference staff at the Library of Congress. Selections are not annotated; however, there are links to other virtual reference sites, including the Internet Public Library and Librarian's Internet Index sites and "Alcove 9," an annotated list of resources compiled by the Library of Congress Humanities and Social Sciences Division subject specialists (available at http://www.loc.gov/rr/main/alcove9/).

6.   LibrarySpot
      http://www.libraryspot.com

Published by StartSpot MediaWorks (Evanston, Illinois), LibrarySpot offers quick links to libraries, reading material, and freely available reference works (arranged by category). Only the briefest (one sentence) descriptions of resources are given, but there is a nice assortment of reference sources (reviewed by an editorial team, according to the site, "for their exceptional quality, content and utility").[6]

7.   Refdesk.com: Reference Desk
       http://refdesk.com/refdsk.html

Refdesk.com is the brainchild of Bob Drudge and represents his personal attempt, underway since 1995, "to bring some semblance of order to the chaos of the Internet."[7] In contrast to the cluttered and somewhat overwhelming main page of Refdesk.com, the Reference Desk page offers a clean listing of sources neatly organized into 32 categories. There are also links to "Essential Reference Tools," "Fast Facts," and more.

These seven portals show different approaches to building useful, free reference collections on the Web. It may be a bit too intense to visit all of these at once. Explore them at your own pace, taking time to note the organization and search capabilities at each site. Enjoy delving into the freely available reference sources that catch your eye. You will find that there is considerable overlap, with some Web sites popping up again and again, but each reference portal also offers some unique sources all its own.

If you want to read further about the shift of reference collections to the Web, a recent, readable resource is the *The Reference Collection: From the Shelf to the Web*, edited by William J. Frost (Haworth Press, 2006; published simultaneously as *The Reference Librarian,* vol. 44, nos. 91/92). This volume includes 16 articles on reference sources on the Web, which discuss issues related to Web-based resources in different types of libraries and offer lists of useful sources in the humanities, science, medicine, social sciences, business, and education. The final article, by Lori Morse, lists the "100 Best Free Reference Web Sites" (based in large part on the MARS lists).

Of course, by the time a reference source appears on a list of the "100 Best," it's old news! How can you stay on top of the latest, greatest sources to hit the Web? Morse (2005) suggests keeping up to date by subscribing to such sources as the Librarians' Internet Index "New This Week," which describes 30–60 selected Web sites each week. You can subscribe by e-mail or by RSS feed (see http://lii.org/pub/htdocs/ subscribe.htm). If you subscribe to the Internet Scout Project's *Scout Report* (available at http://scout.wisc.edu/About/subscribe.php), you will receive weekly e-mails listing 20 or so current Web resources that are of general interest, of interest to researchers and educators, or simply "in the news." Gary Price's Resource Shelf (http:// www.resourceshelf.com) is another longstanding site, now in blog format, that offers not only a weekly newsletter, but also the ability to use RSS feeds for updates.

DEVELOPING REFERENCE WEB PAGES AT YOUR OWN LIBRARY

As you explore the freely available reference sources at the sites listed in the previous section, you'll undoubtedly run across some sources that look like they will be quite useful to your patrons, and to you in your work as a librarian. Perhaps you see a few sources that you wish you'd known about last week or last month. That *Stanford*

Encyclopedia of Philosophy (http://plato.stanford.edu/contents.html) would've been a great resource for the high school honors student who was writing a paper on Socrates the other day; FunTrivia.com (http://www.funtrivia.com) could have added a whole new dimension to the Family Fun Night your library hosted last week. Suddenly, you may find yourself starting to bookmark your favorite sites and organizing these "favorites" into folders.

If possible, try taking these favorite reference sites a step further, using them to enrich the pages on your library's Web site. As of 2006, about 99 percent of public libraries in the United States (and virtually all public school and academic libraries) had Internet access[8]; however, the condition of their Web pages (and the amount of control individual libraries have over these pages) varies greatly. John Carlo Bertot and Charles McClure, who have studied public libraries' Internet connectivity since 1994, note that the most successfully networked public libraries "view their website as an additional branch or as a virtual branch."[9] The library's Web site is the *centerpiece* of its virtual services, as is control over the content of the Web site.[10] Even in a very small branch setting, where perhaps you are "piggybacking" on a central library or a library system Web site, you should have the ability to make suggestions and recommendations with regard to the content of the Web site that your patrons rely on.

Because the needs of your patrons shape your collections, there are no rules set in stone as to what you should include on your Web site. At a minimum, however, your library (or library system) should offer access to the online catalog and a list of available subscription databases along with information about the library itself (such as location, hours, contact information, and a calendar of events). Bertot and McClure (2006) suggest that the most successfully networked libraries will also include links to community information and resources, government information, and other types of sources.[11]

Among the types of reference sources that libraries most commonly choose to link to from their Web sites are directories (including telephone and zip code directories), dictionaries and thesauri, government and political information sources, educational information sources (colleges and universities, information on financial aid), and newspapers.[12] Of course, many other valuable types of information are included on library reference pages: encyclopedias, geographical sources, health and medical sources, business sources, statistical sources, and resources for job seekers and career changers. The list goes on!

As you consider which reference sources you might like to include on your library's Web pages, take a look around at neighboring libraries to see what they have done. Even very small libraries can enhance the value of their pages by adding relevant, useful material. For instance, the Harlan County Public Libraries Reference (Kentucky) provides a simple, yet attractive and locally tailored list of reference sources at http://www.harlancountylibraries.org/reference1.htm. The Viola Public Library (Wisconsin) offers drop-down access to general reference sources, as well as many of local interest, at http://www.swls.org/member.vi.html. The Aztec Public Library (New Mexico) carefully categorizes reference sources the staff believes will be useful for adults, teens, and children, at http://www.azteclibrary.org. (For more ideas, follow some of the links in Andrea Mercado's "Public Library Research Link Collections" (*Public Libraries,* November/December 2003).[13]

You don't have to "reinvent the wheel" on your Web site. Note, for instance, that Harlan County site links to the Kentucky Virtual Library and its virtual reference desk, and the Viola Public Library includes Badgerlink ("Wisconsin's connection to the world of information") as one of its top links. Your job is to provide access to resources that will be of value to patrons in your particular community, making as much use as possible of the support your state or regional library consortium offers, while speaking up for your library's users.

A final word on developing those reference Web pages: make 'em usable! Remember, your goal is to connect people with information, not to hide the information. While the ins and outs of Web site design are beyond the scope of this book, it may be useful to remember "usability guru" Jakob Nielsen's mandates to make your Web site's purpose clear; help your users find what they need; show your Web site's content; and use graphics to enhance (rather than define) your design.[14] Read through Nielsen's "Top Ten Guidelines for Homepage Usability" (http://www.useit.com/alertbox/20020512.html) and avoid his "Top Ten Web Design Mistakes" (http://www.useit.com/alertbox/design mistakes.html). More information on designing usable Web pages can be found in such sources as Steve Krug's *Don't Make Me Think! A Common Sense Approach to Web Usability* (2nd edition); Nielsen's own *Designing Web Usability: The Practice of Simplicity;* or the U.S. government's *Research-based Web Design & Usability Guidelines* (which is freely available at http://www.usability.gov/pdfs/guidelines.html). It's also increasingly important to consider ways to make public library Web pages fully accessible to people with disabilities (again, this is beyond the scope of this book, but definitely worth considering).

OFFERING REFERENCE SERVICES OVER THE WEB

A final way of using the Web to help your patrons find information is to offer them personalized reference service over the Web. At a basic level, you can use the library's Web site as a billboard, posting hours of operation, names of staff, and contact information such as an address and telephone number. But the Web is a highly interactive tool; moving to a higher level of service, you will undoubtedly want to provide an e-mail address so that your patrons can e-mail you their queries.

Libraries have been providing e-mail reference service to patrons since the early 1980s.[15] As more people began using e-mail, more libraries began offering e-mail services to their patrons. Today, it is standard practice for libraries to provide an e-mail address as a point of contact; many libraries (especially larger ones) provide e-mail forms for patrons who have reference questions. A carefully constructed form can help people express their information needs more fully, which allows the reference librarian (in the absence of an in-person reference interview) to gain a deeper understanding of what kind of information might be useful to them. A form can also prompt a patron to provide alternate points of contact (for example, a phone number), in case you feel a conversation would help you better understand their needs. Give some thought to whether it would make sense for your library to offer an e-mail form for reference service. Examples of well-made forms are available at the Internet Public Library (see http://www.ipl.org/div/askus/) and many other libraries as well (see, for instance, the forms at the Jefferson County Public library in Colorado [http://jefferson.lib.co.us/vref.html] and the Irving Public Library in Texas [http://cityofirving.org/library/forms/adultrefquery.html]).

For the past decade or so, instant messaging (or "chatting") has been a popular means of communication, particularly among teenagers and young adults. A few libraries began introducing live chat reference service for their patrons in the late 1990s. It soon became apparent that this kind of service was easily shared among libraries: you didn't have to work in a particular library to "chat" with its patrons and assist them, and so librarians were able to divide up the work involved in offering a new service to their patrons, with each library contributing perhaps a few hours a week of "chatting" librarians in return for many more hours of coverage for their patrons. Several statewide "Ask a Librarian" consortia emerged, and OCLC soon got involved as well, offering chat service (now known as QuestionPoint) drawing on an international consortium of libraries and their librarians. Another popular chat service (Ask A Librarian) is coordinated by Tutor.com, which offers libraries various collaborative staffing options including access to reference assistance in Spanish.[16]

Chat reference service taps into a form of communicating that is comfortable for many people. It allows librarians to provide *immediate* assistance to patrons who are online, no matter where they are physically located—perhaps at the very moment they are using the library's Web pages and experience a moment of confusion. The more sophisticated chat services, such as QuestionPoint, offer librarians the ability to browse through online resources together, to "push" pages onto a patron's computer screen for their consideration, and to e-mail a transcript of the interaction to the patron once they are finished chatting.[17]

Some state libraries have now joined forces with QuestionPoint and Tutor.com or have purchased other software for statewide use, allowing all residents the opportunity to chat online with librarians. Others offer statewide e-mail reference service. Examples of such services include AskColorado (www.askcolorado.org), AnswerXpress in Idaho (www.answerxpress.com), Ohio's KnowItNow (http://www.knowitnow.org), and L-net: Oregon Libraries Network (http://www.oregonlibraries.net).[18] It's important to know what chat services are available to people in your state, so you can link to them from your library's homepage and explore how you might become involved with these initiatives. For a good introduction to virtual reference services in public libraries, see Janet Clapp and Angela Pfeil's article "Virtually Seamless: Exploring the Role of Virtual Public Librarians."[19]

Aside from the formal chat and e-mail consortia described here, a number of libraries have recently been experimenting with the provision of low-cost instant messaging (or IM) service to their patrons. America Online's Instant Messenger (AIM), Yahoo! Messenger, MSN Messenger, and Google Talk are all freely available for download (more options are available for exploration at http://dmoz.org/Computers/ Software/Internet/Clients/Chat/Instant_Messaging). Set up a screen name for your library's reference service, and you're good to go. You can also use Meebo Me (http:// www.meebome.com) to embed IM capability right on your Web site.

Although instant messaging is very basic (it doesn't allow for co-browsing or page-pushing), some librarians believe this is a quick, easy, low-cost way[20] to reach out to some of their patrons, especially high school students and undergrads, for at least a few hours a day. For more information on IM reference services, check out Aaron Schmidt and Michael Stephens's article "IM Me" in *Library Journal* (it includes a list of some libraries including public libraries that offer IM service).[21]

No matter how you offer service, in person, over the phone, via e-mail, or by chatting with your patrons, remember that your main goals are to make your patrons feel welcome to ask questions, understand what their information needs are, and help them to resolve those needs. The ALA Reference & User Services Association (RUSA) Behavioral Guidelines (http://www.ala.org/ala/rusa/protools/referenceguide/guidelines behavioral.cfm) discussed in Chapter 2 apply not only to face-to-face encounters with your patrons but to all modes of reference service. In fact, for each area (Approachability, Interest, Listening/Inquiring, Searching, and Follow Up) RUSA describes specifically how librarians can provide first-rate service to remote patrons (as well as those who come to the library in person).

IN SUM

We live in an age of information abundance: never before have so many resources been freely available to us. It's wonderful to be able to offer library patrons online access to reference sources, to organize these sources in ways that add value, and to use e-mail or chat to extend our services over the Web. Regardless of the media we use to provide service to library users, the bottom line remains constant: to add our expertise and a personal touch to their search for information.

REVIEW

1. What are three different techniques for finding out about useful new Web sites without doing a Web search?
2. Look at the current entries in the Scout Report, Resource Shelf, and LII: New This Week. Are any of the sites worth bookmarking for future reference?

3. Using the reference portals discussed in this chapter, find 10 sources you did not know about previously that would benefit patrons in your library. What would be the best way to notify them about such resources?

4. Does your library have the demand and the resources to develop its own Web page of reference sources? If so, what might the main categories be? If not, how might you direct your users to other reference portals from your library's Web site?

5. Of the Web-based reference services discussed in this chapter—e-mail forms, chat, and instant messaging—which do you think would work best for the community your library serves? Would it be practical to implement a new form of service in your library?

6. Does your state offer virtual reference service that you can link to from your library's Web site?

7. Having skimmed the design guides referred to in this chapter, take a fresh look at your library's Web site. Are there any steps you can take to make it more usable?

NOTES

1. Cybrarian. *Merriam-Webster online* (free version). Available online at http://www. m-w.com/dictionary/cybrarian

2. American Library Association, Machine Assisted Reference Section (2007). Criteria for selection of MARS Best Reference Websites. Available online at http://www.ala.org/ala/ rusa/rusaourassoc/rusasections/mars/marspubs/marsbestrefcriteria.htm

3. Internet Public Library (2001). The Internet Public Library mission statement. Available online at http://www.ipl.org/div/about/newmission.html

4. Internet Public Library: Reference (2007). Available online at http://www.ipl.org/div/ subject/browse/ref00.00.00

5. Librarian's Internet Index (2007). LII Selection Criteria. Available online at http://lii. org/pub/htdocs/selectioncriteria.htm

6. About LibrarySpot.com. (1997–2007). Available online at http://www.libraryspot.com/ about.htm

7. Drudge, B. (2005). My Virtual Reference Desk. Available online at http://refdesk.com/ mission.html

8. Bertot, J.C., McClure, C.R., Jaeger, P.T., & Ryan, J. *Public libraries and the Internet 2006: Study results and findings.* Prepared for the Bill and Melinda Gates Foundation and the American Library Association. Tallahassee: Florida State University Information Use Management and Policy Institute. Available online at http://www.ii.fsu.edu/plinternet_reports.cfm; U.S. Dept of Education (2005). *Digest of education statistics 2005.* Available online at http://nces.ed.gov/programs/digest/d05/

9. Bertot et al., *Public libraries*, p. 3.

10. ibid., p. 124.

11. ibid., p. 177.

12. Sowards, S. (2005). Structures and choices for ready reference Web sites. *Reference Librarian, 44*(91/92), 117–38.

13. Mercado, A. (2003). Public library research link collections. *Public Libraries, 42*, 360–61. Available online at http://www.ala.org/ala/pla/plapubs/publiclibraries/42n6.pdf

14.   Nielsen, J. (2002). Top Ten Guidelines for Homepage Usability. Available online at http://www.useit.com/alertbox/20020512.html

15.   Schardt, C.M. (1983). Electronic mail service: Applications in the Pacific Northwest Region. *Bulletin of the Medical Library Association, 71,* 437–38.

16.   QuestionPoint 24/7 reference service. (2005). Available online at http://questionpoint.org; Tutor.com. Ask A Librarian (2006). Available online at http://www.tutor.com/products/aal.aspx

17.   QuestionPoint 24/7 reference service. (2005). Available online at http://questionpoint.org

18.   A state-by-state list is available in appendix 7 of Bertot et al. (2006).

19.   Clapp, J., & Pfeil, A. (2005). Virtually seamless: Exploring the role of virtual public librarians. *Public Libraries, 44,* 95–100.

20.   Houghton, S., & Schmidt, A. (2005). Web-based chat vs. instant messaging: Who wins? *Online, 29*(4), 26–30.

21.   Schmidt, A., & Stephens, M. (2005). IM me. *Library Journal, 130*(6), 34–35.

CHAPTER 10

Reference Ethics
and Reference Policies

I worry far more about decisions based on ignorance than those based on information.[1]

When we worry about doing the right thing in a particular situation, or wonder if our actions are helpful or harmful, we are asking ethical questions. Ethics address questions of principles and values; they deal with "what is morally good and bad, right and wrong."[2] Naturally, we all ask these kinds of philosophical questions as individuals, and as members of our larger society. Those of us who work in libraries must also ask these questions as members of the library profession. What does it mean to "do the right thing" as an information professional?

OUR PROFESSIONAL ETHICS: VALUES, GUIDELINES, AND CODES

Chances are, you are not working in a library because you want to "get rich quick" or to become powerful or famous. Instead, I'm guessing, you were drawn to the library because you care about your community and see ways in which your work can help people learn and grow and expand their horizons. Libraries exist to serve their communities by supporting the informational, educational, and entertainment needs of the people in those communities.[3] By working in a library, you are supporting this mission. You're also tapping into a deeper set of values on which the library profession rests including access to information, preservation of information, intellectual freedom, democracy and diversity, education and lifelong learning, confidentiality and privacy, professionalism and service, social responsibility, and concern for the public good.[4]

As reference professionals, we can certainly see our commitment to access to information, intellectual freedom, and service in the RUSA Guidelines for Behavioral Performance (http://www.ala.org/ala/rusa/protools/referenceguide/guidelinesbehavioral. cfm), which I have discussed in depth elsewhere in this book. These guidelines remind us of the importance of welcoming our patrons to the library; understanding their needs; performing effective, accurate searches for information; and ensuring, to the best of our abilities, that their needs have been met.

At a more general level, and bearing in mind the professional values of librarianship, the American Library Association has developed a Code of Ethics to help guide our actions, particularly in moments of conflict. The principles of this Code of Ethics are expressed as follows:

I.   We provide the highest level of service to all library users through appropriate and usefully organized resources; equitable service policies; equitable access; and accurate, unbiased, and courteous responses to all requests.

II.   We uphold the principles of intellectual freedom and resist all efforts to censor library resources.

III.   We protect each library user's right to privacy and confidentiality with respect to information sought or received and resources consulted, borrowed, acquired, or transmitted.

IV.   We recognize and respect intellectual property rights.

V.   We treat co-workers and other colleagues with respect, fairness and good faith, and advocate conditions of employment that safeguard the rights and welfare of all employees of our institutions.

VI.   We do not advance private interests at the expense of library users, colleagues, or our employing institutions.

VII.   We distinguish between our personal convictions and professional duties and do not allow our personal beliefs to interfere with fair representation of the aims of our institutions or the provision of access to their information resources.

VIII.   We strive for excellence in the profession by maintaining and enhancing our own knowledge and skills, by encouraging the professional development of co-workers, and by fostering the aspirations of potential members of the profession.[5]

How does this code relate, specifically, to our provision of reference service? According to Charles A. Bunge, a longtime reference philosopher, it is reference librarians' "direct service to individual clients" that distinguishes our work; thus it follows that our responsibility to these clients is at the heart of our ethical concerns.[6]

Bunge believes that as the librarian and the patron work together as an information-seeking team of sorts, they share responsibility for making decisions along the way. The librarian is generally more knowledgeable about the resources available and the use of search strategies to locate appropriate information, and has more authority in this realm; however, "the librarian does not have expertise in the inquirer's values, in how the information should be used, or in the inquirer's goals in life."[7] In these areas, the patron holds the responsibility for making decisions. In his mind, **professional competence** is the most important ethical obligation of reference librarians. This involves the efficient provision of accurate, appropriate information as well as *not* providing information the librarian is not qualified to provide.

Professional competence relates closely to statements I and VIII in the ALA Code of Ethics. Item I covers our responsibility for providing courteous, accurate, unbiased, and equitable service (drawing on a strong collection of resources), and VIII addresses our need to stay up-to-date with the field and continually expand our knowledge. With regard to the importance of knowing our limits as information providers, it's worth noting that RUSA (the Reference and User Services Association of the ALA) has also put together a set of guidelines for medical, legal, and business responses, available at http://www.ala.org/ala/rusa/protools/referenceguide/guidelinesmedical.cfm.[8] These guidelines emphasize the need for libraries to provide access to current, accurate, authoritative sources and assistance in their use—as well as the need to refer questions that fall outside the boundaries of librarians' expertise (we may be information experts, but the great majority of us are *not* doctors, lawyers, or investment bankers!).

The medical, legal, and business guidelines also highlight the importance of **tact and confidentiality** when answering sensitive questions. In fact, treating all kinds of information requests confidentially is fundamental in reference work. This relates to item III of the ALA Code of Ethics, which asserts "each library user's right to privacy and confidentiality." If you feel a question is best answered by consulting with another librarian, good professional practice is to ask the patron's permission to bring someone else into the interaction, or to ask a colleague for assistance without revealing your patron's identity. Some patrons are open and sharing; they ask their questions openly and loudly, and invite every passerby to join in the hunt for information. That's fine, as long as it's the patron who initiates the sharing. Other people are more hesitant to share their information needs, and of course, you do not want to violate their trust in you by broadcasting their personal business to the world. This includes maintaining confidentiality with regard to the sources your patrons consult.

Intellectual freedom is another important guiding principle of librarianship (evident in items II and VII of the Code of Ethics). In terms of reference service, this means that we are committed to building strong, balanced reference collections that reflect the needs of our community whether or not these happen to coincide with our personal needs or interests. It also means that we strive to answer a wide variety of reference questions to the best of our abilities, even questions we may find personally upsetting or offensive, as long as they fall within the boundaries of the law.

Lots of debate has gone on about the extent to which reference librarians should maintain a commitment to intellectual freedom when there are obvious conflicts between their obligation to a particular client and their obligations to others in the community. In a 1976 experiment that has become famous in the library world, Robert Hauptman went to 13 public and academic libraries asking for information on how to construct a small bomb, which, he hinted, would be used to blow up a house. None of the librarians refused to cooperate on ethical grounds; in fact, most of them tried to help him find the information.[9] Similar experiments (where the questions have been about how to freebase cocaine, or even how to commit suicide) have met with similar helpful responses from librarians.[10]

Where do we draw the line with regard to providing access to information? Even the authors of the studies mentioned here are in disagreement, with Hauptman appalled by the apparent lack of social responsibility shown by the librarians, and Robert Dowd (the author of the cocaine study) supporting the patron's right to freely access this information. It is clear that librarians must operate within the law so that if a patron is requesting access to child pornography, for instance, they are legally and morally obligated to refuse him or her service. But what about those questions that fall within a fuzzy, gray area? In these cases, we are forced to weigh our responsibility to the patron against our responsibility to the broader community, or to the library as an organization.

Charles Bunge suggests that it may help us to remember the basic values of a democratic society such as honesty, respecting human dignity and worth, and protecting people from injury by others.[11] He believes that if you have *clear reason* to think that a patron will make use of information to harm others, you could ethically choose to refuse assistance to him or her. Another reference librarian, John Swan, however, notes the likelihood of someone with criminal intentions openly asking for information is relatively small, while the dangers of living in a world of "suspicious and censorious librarians" may be greater than we suspect.[12] Sometimes, we are forced to make tough decisions about what it truly means to be ethical.

Closely related to the idea of intellectual freedom is the ideal of offering our patrons **equitable service and access** to information (item I in the ALA Code of Ethics). Public libraries, in particular, are institutions that strive to provide information to *all* people in the community regardless of who they are, where they're from, or the views they hold.[13] This is a noble ideal and an important one in a democratic society, but it can also be difficult to uphold. To follow this guideline properly, we need to provide the same level of service to the almighty mayor as we do to the mentally ill woman who asks us the same set of annoying questions day after day; we need to offer as much respect and assistance to the surly 13-year-old who resents the school assignment he's being forced to complete as we do the bright, handsome young lawyer who's just moved to town. We need to find ways of supporting those who have limited access to information resources outside of the library, to help put them on an equal footing with those who have plenty.

Finally, we need to consider the role of the reference librarian with regard to **intellectual property** (item IV in the Code of Ethics). Respect for intellectual property is not just a professional issue; it is also a legal one. Section 106 of the 1976 Copyright Act gives the author(s) of an original work (or the people authorized by them) the exclusive rights to reproduce that work, distribute copies, produce derivative works, and publicly perform or display the work.[14] There are certain exceptions to this right, one of the most important being the doctrine of "fair use" (laid out in section 107 of the Copyright Act). Fair use permits the reproduction of works under certain circumstances depending on:

1. the purpose and character of the use, including whether such use is of commercial nature or is for nonprofit educational purposes;
2. the nature of the copyrighted work;
3. amount and substantiality of the portion used in relation to the copyrighted work as a whole; and
4. the effect of the use upon the potential market for or value of the copyrighted work.[15]

As with the intellectual freedom issue discussed previously, there are times when you may be called on to make a judgment call as to whether it is legitimate to make a copy of a book, a CD, or a computer file. Although there are no hard and fast rules, the courts tend to consider cases in which people are reproducing small bits of copyrighted works for educational (or nonprofit) reasons, that will have little or no effect on the market value of the work, as constituting "fair use." On the other hand, if a patron asks you to help her copy every single page of the *Concise Encyclopedia of Investing* so that she will not have to go out and buy it, it's a good bet that's not fair use. It's important to be aware of the kinds of copies you're allowed to make for your patrons as well as your responsibilities regarding interlibrary loan; and although you're *not* the "copyright police," you should have a sign by the copy machine stating that making copies "may be subject to the copyright law."[16]

TWENTY-FIRST CENTURY ETHICAL DILEMMAS

In our current environment, in which information is increasingly being made available in digital format on the Internet, some new ethical issues have arisen and some old ones have intensified. Richard Rubin, a professor of Library & Information Science at Kent State University who frequently has written about ethics in the field, believes that our current computer technologies "may encourage or even promote unethical conduct."[17] Our network of computers offers us relative anonymity; the possibility of speedy, remote access; quick and easy copying options; and the ability to readily reach a large audience. All of this, he believes, makes thoughtful ethical reflection more important than ever.

In the spirit of reflection, let's think some more about the areas of importance to reference librarians that we just reviewed, focusing this time on our digital networked world:

Professional competence: Reference librarians must be able to provide excellent service not only in person, but also via e-mail and chat. We're also challenged to stay abreast of constantly changing resources and search technologies, which makes our lives more interesting, but a bit more stressful as well.

Privacy and confidentiality: Our patrons' digital footprints (and ours) are everywhere. We must think carefully about how to keep e-mail and chat communication with patrons confidential and how to "wipe clean" the trails that are left after people have consulted databases and other resources in the library or even after they've simply signed up to use a computer in the reference area, in order to maintain their privacy.

Intellectual freedom: Widespread access to the Internet has greatly increased people's access to all kinds of information, including pornography, scenes of extreme violence, and other types of controversial materials. What kind of information is it appropriate for people to access from within the library? How might this vary according to age group? Who should be held responsible for the types of materials patrons access?

It is especially important for library staff to carefully consider the pros and cons of filtering the Internet and to be aware of the current state of filtering technology. The American Library Association officially considers filtering to be a form of censorship; it points to the fact that filtering technology is imperfect, letting material that it is set to block flow through in some cases and shutting out "inoffensive" Web sites in other cases.[18] The U.S. government, on the other hand, requires that any library receiving federal funding such as a discounted e-rate connection to the Internet, or funding from an LSTA (Library Services and Technology Act) grant must install filters on its computers.[19] It also includes, however, a provision for the libraries to disable the filter when asked to do so. Keeping up with current laws that affect our library's services, as well as current technologies, is an ongoing challenge.

Equitable service and access: Libraries are committed to offering their patrons free access to computers, but what about related services, such as printing? Does charging for printing set up an economic barrier for the schoolchild from an impoverished family who needs to use the library's computers to research, type, and then print out her paper for health class? If we filter the Internet in the children and young adults section of the library so that she isn't able to retrieve the full range of information on her chosen paper topic of "breast cancer," are we further discriminating on the basis of age?

Intellectual property: In our fluid, online environment, our patrons can download articles from databases, copy files, and cut and paste with the stroke of a key. It's all so easy! Where do our responsibilities lie in all of this? When we work with patrons, we can help them understand the difference between what is *possible* and what is ethical or legal. Recognizing that plagiarism is a widespread phenomenon, it is especially important to explain this concept to children and young adults,[20] reinforcing what their teachers are undoubtedly telling them in the classroom. We need to be aware of the legality of our own copying practices as well, and, if we provide e-mail or chat reference service, to maintain awareness of our licensing agreements for online databases (understanding exactly who has legal access to them).

REFERENCE POLICIES

Documents such as the ALA's list of Core Values and Code of Ethics are important foundations for the library profession, but they are also abstract and philosophical and don't always make it easy to figure out a practical course of action. To bring some of these lofty principles down to earth for everyday problem-solving purposes, librarians create policies. In developing their policies, librarians must take into account the needs of their users, the mission of the library, the values of the profession, and the society in which we all live.[21]

With regard to reference services, at a minimum libraries should have a reference collection development policy in place (either independently or as a part of the larger collection development policy) both to guide the collection management process and to turn to in case there are challenges that threaten intellectual freedom. Most reference collection development policies address the purpose of the collection and the criteria for selection and deselection. They may go into detail about specific sources as well. An example of a carefully developed reference collection policy, in place at the Morton Grove Public Library in Illinois, is available at http://www.webrary.org/inside/colldevadultref.html.

Some libraries have reference service policies as well that specify the types of service the library is prepared to offer. See, for instance, the sample policy developed by the Outagamie Waupaca Library System in Wisconsin for its member libraries, at http://www.owlsweb.info/L4L/policies/X.asp

In the number of useful books on creating library policies, Rebecca Brumley's *The Reference Librarian's Policies, Forms, Guidelines, and Procedures Handbook: With CD-ROM* (New York: Neal-Schuman, 2006) specifically deals with reference policies. More general works include Richard Wood and Frank Hoffmann's *Library Collection Development Policies: Academic, Public, and Special Libraries* (Scarecrow Press, 2005) and Sandra Nelson and June Garcia's *Creating Policies for Results: From Chaos to Clarity* (Chicago: ALA, 2003).

Additional useful general policy links for reference librarians are available at the OWLS Web site listed previously (http://www.owlsweb.info/L4L/policies.asp). The State Library of Ohio has provided a number of helpful sample statements, at http://winslo.state.oh.us/publib/policies.html, and it's quite possible that your state library or regional consortium has done the same. Finally, the American Library Association also offers an interesting compilation of Intellectual Freedom statements and policies, at http://www.ala.org/ala/oif/statementspols/statementspolicies.htm. There are links to many of the core philosophical documents of librarianship at this site as well.

IN SUM

It's not always easy to figure out the "right" way to handle a controversial question or a tricky access issue. Deepening our understanding of some of the values librarians hold dear, understanding the ethical stances that we may be asked to take, and developing practical policies that we can turn to in a moment of need can help make our responsibilities clearer and make our jobs easier.

REVIEW

Bearing in mind your professional responsibilities (as laid out in the ALA Code of Ethics), how might you respond to the following situations?

1. A local high school English teacher who serves on the library's board of trustees has prevailed on the library to help develop a wiki of local resources with her Honors English class. The library director thinks it's a great idea, and punts the project over to you. You don't know the first thing about developing a wiki, although you've looked at plenty of articles in *Wikipedia* and find the idea interesting. How do you proceed, keeping in mind your ethical obligation of professional competence?

2. You notice a "regular" patron, a high school student who always comes in alone, repeatedly looking at sites that seem to glorify the Columbine high school killings, in plain view of your desk. One day he asks you for help in obtaining a book called *Blind-Sided: Homicide Where It Is Least Expected,* via interlibrary loan. Should you order the book for him, even though you are concerned he might be planning a violent act? Should you contact his parents?

3. The wife of your town's police chief asks you to help her locate resources for battered women. She seems nervous and looks like she may have been crying. Should you reach out to her and ask if anything's wrong at home?

4. A quiet older gentleman comes into the library every afternoon and always asks to have the filter deactivated on his computer. On more than one occasion you field angry complaints from parents, who tell you their kids can see him looking at pornographic images and videos as they walk past. Can you satisfy the concerned parents without restricting the man's intellectual freedom? Does your Internet use policy give you any guidance in this matter?

5. A clean-cut young man enters the library holding a pamphlet called *Who Runs the Media? The Alarming Facts,* published by the American Nazi Party, and demands

that you include it in your library's collection. Are you obligated to do so? How can your library's collection policy assist you in handling this request?

6. The same man also wants to know about reserving the library's public meeting rooms once a week for his "study group." According to the ALA Code of Ethics, is he entitled to a room? If you grant his request, what will you say to people who are appalled that the library is playing host to a racist organization?

7. You're helping a middle school student research her term paper using a variety of electronic resources. You step away to help others; when you check back with her you see her copy and paste two paragraphs from the *Encarta* article "Unemployment" into a Word document entitled, "Social studies report for Mr. Thomas." How might you tactfully address the issue of plagiarism with her?

NOTES

1. Broderick, D. (1982, summer). Value laden barriers to information dissemination. *The Reference Librarian, 4,* 19–23.
2. *Encyclopædia Britannica Online,* s.v. "Ethics." (2007). http://search.eb.com.libaccess. sjlibrary.org/eb/article-9106054 (retrieved June 20, 2007).
3. Rubin, R. (2004*). Foundations of Library & Information Science* (2nd ed.) New York: Neal Schuman, pp. 297–98.
4. American Library Association. (2004). *Core values statement.* Available online at http://www. ala.org/ala/oif/statementspols/corevaluesstatement/corevalues.htm
5. American Library Association (2005). *Code of ethics.* Available online at http://www. ala.org/ala/oif/statementspols/codeofethics/codeethics.htm
6. Bunge, C.A. (1999/1990). Ethics and the reference librarian. *The Reference Librarian, 66,* 25–43, p. 26.
7. ibid., p. 28.
8. Reference & User Services Association. (2001). *Guidelines for medical, legal, and business responses.* Available online at http://www.ala.org/ala/rusa/protools/referenceguide/ guidelinesmedical.cfm
9. Hauptman, R. (1976). Professionalism or culpability? An experiment in ethics. *Wilson Library Bulletin, 50,* 626–27.
10. Dowd, R.C. (1989). I want to find out how to freebase cocaine, or yet another unobtrusive test of reference performance. *The Reference Librarian, 25/26,* 483–93; Juznic, P., Urbanija, J., Grabrijan, E., Miklavc, S., Oslaj, D., & Svoljsak, S. (2001). Excuse me, how do I commit suicide? Access to ethically disputed items of information in public libraries. *Library Management, 22,* 75–80.
11. Bunge, "Ethics and the reference librarian."
12. Swan, J.C. (1982). Ethics at the reference desk: Comfortable theories and tricky practices. *The Reference Librarian, 4,* p. 113.
13. American Library Association (1996). *Library Bill of Rights.* Available online at http:// www.ala.org/ala/oif/statementspols/statementsif/librarybillrights.htm
14. U.S. Copyright Office (2006). *Circular 1: Copyright Office basics.* Available online at http://www.copyright.gov/circs/circ1.html
15. U.S. Copyright Office (2006). *FL-102: Fair use.* Available online at http://www.copyright. gov/fls/fl102.html. Stanford University's Copyright & Fair Use site, available online at

http://fairuse.stanford.edu/Copyright_and_Fair_Use_Overview, is also a very useful resource.

16.   U.S. Copyright Office. Copyright law, Chapter 1 (section 108(f)(1)). Available online at http://www.copyright.gov/title17/92chap1.html#108

17.   Rubin, *Foundations of Library*, p. 353.

18.   American Library Association (2007). Filters and filtering. Available online at http://www.ala.org/ala/oif/ifissues/filtersfiltering.htm

19.   U.S. Supreme Court (2003). *United States et al. v. American Library Association, Inc. et al.* Available online at http://www.supremecourtus.gov/opinions/boundvolumes/539bv.pdf

20.   Sharkey, J.R., & Culp, F.B. (2005). Cyberplagiarism and the library: Issues and solutions. *Reference Librarian, 44* (91/92), 103–16.

21.   Rubin, *Foundations of Library*.

CHAPTER 11

Networking with Other Libraries and Librarians

The library should not only be a depository of information, it should be a place of community—the town square that once was.[1]

We live in an increasingly interconnected world. You can make a positive difference in this world by helping people connect with the information they need when they need it. To do so effectively, you need to cultivate your "people" skills—that is, develop your talent for working with patrons, library employees and volunteers, the library board, local government officials, and others in the broader library community (and, I hope, take pleasure in it!).[2] This doesn't mean you have to be some sort of social butterfly, or even an extravert. It simply means you need to have confidence in reaching out to members of your local community, on the one hand, and to members of the library community, on the other.

YOUR ROLE IN THE LOCAL COMMUNITY

In their 1988 *Handbook for Small, Rural, and Emerging Public Libraries,* Anne Gervasi and Betty Kay Seibt wrote: "What makes a library is not its building but its services. A library is really no more than the services it offers and is no more effective than how well those services meet the needs of the library's public."[3]

Twenty years later, these words still ring true. Now, as then, your library exists to provide the community with access to information and to offer programs and services that will support the educational, cultural, recreational, and research needs of your community. In many communities the library also provides an important meeting space, a gathering spot for groups and a logical location for activities of different sorts.

In some ways, it's easier than ever for libraries to fulfill these social and informational needs. Connecting to the Internet and being able to offer public access to it have been extremely beneficial for many small-town and rural libraries over the past decade. This kind of "networking" has made libraries more visible in their communities, attracted new patrons, and enabled library staff to enhance and expand their reference services and to offer access to a wealth of information.[4]

It has also brought new challenges. Computers and networks malfunction; we need to know basic "technological troubleshooting" techniques and who to call when the problems are beyond our capabilities. Even when everything's working properly, technology changes quickly; we must find ways of keeping up with new developments. And we need to work at personalizing information technology and using it intelligently,[5] tying the services we offer to the needs of our community. This last responsibility may involve going beyond our informal understanding of the community's needs and conducting a more formal community survey to find out what people would like the library to offer.[6]

How do you keep up with this rapidly changing landscape? How can you become more technologically savvy and identify additional sources of technological support? How can you learn new ways to assess your community's needs and come up with fresh ideas for offering reference and information services? Fortunately, you don't have to do this all by yourself. You can draw on the resources of the broader library community, of which you are a member.

YOUR ROLE IN THE LIBRARY COMMUNITY

The library community is a supportive one. Even if you are a "lone librarian," running the show all by yourself in a small town, there are agencies, organizations, and groups of peers who stand ready to lend a hand. They sponsor conferences, workshops, publications, and continuing education opportunities that can help you develop your professional abilities to their fullest.

State Libraries, Regional Consortia, and Local Systems

The state library is a key partner in your efforts to build strong reference services. State libraries play an increasingly important role in supporting libraries. They may offer any or all of the following services:[7]

- Funding, either directly or through grants they have procured
- Network services such as basic Internet connections, statewide virtual libraries and virtual reference services, specialized digital collections, videoconferencing, remote Web site hosting, and organized access to Web-based information (including links to state government and general reference sources)
- Demonstration projects where local libraries can have access to new technologies
- Library directories, newsletters, listservs, and blogs to facilitate communication among librarians within a state and disseminate new information and ideas
- Professional library consultants to help libraries solve problems and implement new services
- Continuing education and training for library staff
- Assistance with data collection and evaluation of services
- Development of regulations, standards, and policies
- Advocacy with government officials, database vendors, and publishers

Your state library's Web site can be a critical resource for learning about state-supported virtual libraries and virtual reference services, workshops of various sorts, free advising and consulting services, and funding opportunities for your library. The Chief Officers of State Library Agencies (COSLA) maintains a directory of links and data for all 50 state libraries (plus two U.S. territories and the District of Columbia) at http://www.cosla.org/profiles/

State libraries also maintain directories listing all of the public libraries and library systems in the state including contact information. If you're part of a county or regional system but are not quite sure who all the other members are or where, exactly, you fit into the picture, your state library can help clarify this for you and can put you in touch with your peers. Some states (such as Minnesota) have well-developed regional consortia whose libraries have been pooling their resources for many years to better serve their patrons (and supporting each other along the way). In other states, libraries coordinate their efforts at a county level. In either case, it makes perfect sense to get to know your fellow librarians and become involved with county, regional, or state-level activities to the extent that you are able.

Library Associations: Your State Library Association, ALA, and ARSL

A good first step for involvement is to join your state library association, if you haven't already. The annual membership fee is usually quite reasonable and often follows a "sliding scale" model (where members pay more or less according to their salaries). State library associations support their members in a variety of ways,[8] including publications, workshops, and usually an annual conference. Most state library associations include special interest groups (or "roundtables"), and invariably there is a group focused on reference services. Joining such a group can be a wonderful way to connect with others who share your interests, as well as your day-to-day challenges, and to forge lasting professional relationships and friendships. Your active participation in the association also means that smaller libraries are represented and that their interests and concerns will not be overlooked.

Special interest groups may meet quarterly or biannually; most state library associations also hold an annual conference in which all members are invited to participate. These conferences can be a lot of fun, as well as being educational. They usually provide a few inspiring speakers and useful sessions on topics of professional interest; sometimes interesting workshops are offered; and there are always vendors from the major library-related companies, ready to display their wares and give away posters and other "freebies."

Attending a conference does involve paying a registration fee, travel expenses, and (sometimes) an overnight hotel room, although most state library associations try to meet in different parts of a state in alternating years. Especially if you work in a small library, however, the annual conference of your state library association can be a valuable experience. Among other things, simply seeing your colleagues in attendance serves as an important reminder that you are not alone, that there are people throughout the state who share your values and your interests (as well as your desire to walk away with some cool, free bookmarks and posters!).

If you are the kind of person who truly enjoys and benefits from conferences, I heartily recommend attending the **American Library Association** annual conference at some point in your career. Frequently more than 20,000 librarians are in attendance, and thousands of exhibitors display the latest technology, sources, and services the field has to offer. The conference features dozens of nationally renowned authors and speakers and hundreds of different programs and sessions to choose from—a myriad of learning opportunities. A listing of future ALA conference locations is available at http://www. ala.org/ala/confservices/upcoming/upcomingconferences.htm

Of course, the annual conference is just one of the American Library Association's many offerings. It is, after all, "the oldest and largest library association in the world,"[9] boasting over 65,000 members. ALA hosts 11 major divisions (including RUSA, the Reference and User Services Association, and PLA, the Public Library Association) and numerous roundtables and committees, including a roundtable for library support staff (LSSIRT, at http://www.ala.org/ala/lssirt/lssirt.htm) and a committee on **rural, native and tribal libraries** (at http://www.ala.org/RuralLibraries).

RUSA, PLA, and LSSIRT offer many opportunities for participation and learning. For instance, the RUSA Web site (www.ala.org/rusa) currently includes links to online professional development courses, RUSA discussion lists, a blog where you can post reference-related thoughts and questions, and a "virtual reference" adventure. Membership in ALA and its divisions also includes subscription to its print publications (such as *American Libraries, RUSQ—Reference & User Services Quarterly,* and *Public Libraries*).

Even if you are not a member of ALA, many of the valuable resources at its Web site (http://www.ala.org) are freely available for your use. We have drawn on some of these, such as the ALA Intellectual Freedom documents, the RUSA Behavioral Guidelines, and RUSA's Outstanding Reference Sources list, in previous chapters. ALA has also developed a gateway to some of the online professional tools that are most useful to librarians in their day-to-day work, including information about literacy, outreach to underserved populations, diversity, intellectual freedom, and other concerns, at http://www.ala.org/ala/proftools/professional.htm.

Another organization to bear in mind is the **Association of Rural and Small Libraries** (ARSL—http://arsl.clarion.edu/) sponsored by Clarion University in Pennsylvania's Center for the Study of Rural Librarianship. Membership includes electronic access to the journal *Rural Libraries,* as well as opportunities to network with others interested in the development of small and rural libraries. There are currently approximately 240 members in the ARSL.[10] Recordings and handouts from the recent (2006) Joint Conference of the Association of Rural and Small Libraries and Association of Bookmobile and Outreach Services are available, at http://www.rurallibraries.org/rboc/.

WebJunction

WebJunction (www.webjunction.org), an important recent initiative funded by the Gates Foundation, OCLC, and other partners, offers a large variety of resources for libraries, with a focus on integrating technology into library services. It features lists of resources, ideas for library projects, online courses, and "webinars" on issues and technologies ranging from information literacy and rural outreach to Web development and network administration. Many of the resources on the site can be accessed for free, but some of the courses require a fee (typically $50). The site also offers columns and blogs from librarians of various stripes, themed discussion forums, and wikis facilitating collaboration on various library issues. If you are in a small or rural library, be sure to visit their special guide at http://webjunction.org/do/DisplayContent?id=1235, and check out their free, self-paced Rural Library Sustainability Online Course (at http://webjunction.org/do/DisplayContent?id=16846). WebJunction has several sites localized to particular states. Check if your state is one, at http://webjunction.org/do/displayCommunityList

Current Awareness Tools: Professional Journals, Lists, and Blogs

Part of library work involves taking time to read about and reflect on some of the issues and new developments in the field. The preceding discussion of various local, state, and national associations and networking opportunities includes references to several publications, blogs, and discussion lists you might want to dip into from time to time.

If you join your state library association, the American Library Association, or the ARSL, you will automatically receive a subscription to their official publication as part of your membership (*American Libraries* and *Rural Libraries,* in the case of the last two associations). For matters related to reference services, three **key journals** are *Reference & User Services Quarterly (RUSQ), Reference Services Review,* and *The Reference Librarian.* Although all are important, *RUSQ* is the least expensive and most widely accessible of the three (through its Web site at http://www.rusq.org and through multiple online databases). If you enjoy automatically receiving the latest news, some journals (including *American Libraries* and *RUSQ*) now offer RSS feeds for stories.

E-mail discussion lists, or **listservs,** are another good way to stay attuned to what's going on in the profession as well as to ask for, and offer, advice on reference work and reference issues. Best of all, they're free! LIBREF-L is a discussion list specifically for reference librarians. Although it sometimes has an emphasis on academic libraries, it can be a great resource for finding out about how to handle tricky reference issues. You can subscribe to this list at http://listserv.kent.edu/scripts/wa.exe?SUBED1=libref-l& A=1. Project Wombat (http://lists.project-wombat.org) is a list where you can freely post "stumpers," questions that you're having a hard time with, and elicit the help of your colleagues in answering them. Or, feel free to jump in and answer a "tough one" yourself.

On a more general level, PUBLIB is an e-mail discussion list for people working in public libraries. The list is quite active, with participants from urban, suburban, and rural libraries across the country. For instructions on subscribing and links to archived discussions, go to http://lists.webjunction.org/publib/. State library agencies and library associations frequently have e-mail lists for their members as well. The degree to which these are participative and useful will vary; fortunately, you can always "unsubscribe" from tiresome lists.

Weblogs, or **blogs,** are becoming an increasingly important means of communication in the library field. Many blogs are personal narratives (or rants), but some professional blogs of note are starting to emerge. ResourceShelf (www.resourceshelf.com) is a blog founded by Gary Price, a library consultant; its reports on new or overlooked Web-based resources are useful. RUSA has a blog (http://www.rusablog.org), as do the Public Library Association (http://www.plablog.org) and WebJunction (http://blog. webjunctionworks.org/). As with some of the journals listed in this chapter, RSS feeds (which can be read using free Web-based services such as BlogLines or Google Reader, or using desktop applications) make it easier to keep up with new postings on the blogs you might be interested in following.

Continuing Education

If you are interested in formally attending a workshop or completing a brief class on a specific topic related to reference, let's say, a brief course on interpersonal communication techniques, searching the Internet, or implementing a virtual reference service, you're in luck! There are many options available to you.

- The American Library Association's page on continuing education includes information about many ALA-sponsored workshops and conferences: http://www.ala.org/ala/education/ce/continuingeducation.htm
- WebJunction maintains an "e-learning clearinghouse," where you can search for continuing education courses and programs to suit your needs: http://www.webjunction.org/do/DisplayContent?id=13651
- The Education Institute (based in Canada) offers online courses, audio conferences, live Web conferences, and face-to-face meetings on all kinds of library-related topics: http://www.thepartnership.ca/partnership/bins/index_ei.asp?cid=83&lang=1
- Some library schools offer online continuing education courses and workshops (you do not have to be admitted to the school to register). For instance:

  - University of Wisconsin-Milwaukee http://www.ed2go.com/uwm/
  - Simmons http://www.simmons.edu/gslis/continuinged/workshops/
  - University of Wisconsin-Madison http://www.slis.wisc.edu/continueed/index.html

Continuing education courses are seldom free, although you may be able to talk your library's administration, or a patron and benefactor of the library, into subsidizing your attendance. There are a few no-cost offerings available. Infopeople (www.infopeople.org), which offers training to employees of California libraries, frequently sponsors workshops on technology, management, collection development, legal issues, and many other topics, delivered online or hosted at various libraries throughout the state. Although enrollment in these valuable sessions is restricted to California librarians, training materials from past workshops (including PowerPoints, handouts, and exercises) are made freely available soon afterwards at http://www.infopeople.org/training/past/. And SirsiDynix, a company that designs software used in many libraries, maintains the SirsiDynix Institute (www.sirsidynixinstitute.com), where it offers free participatory Web seminars on a variety of timely topics. Events are archived (see http://www.sirsidynixinstitute.com/archive.php) and can be freely streamed. You can even subscribe to podcasts of their seminars, if you so desire.

Professional Education Programs

Perhaps the moment has come to pursue (or to complete) a master's degree in library & information science. Thanks to the Internet, even if you live far from a university it's actually possible to earn a master's degree without completely uprooting. If you're playing with the idea of enrolling (online or "in person"), your first step should be to check out the American Library Association's list of accredited graduate programs in Library and Information Studies at http://www.ala.org/ala/accreditation/lisdirb/lisdirectory.htm.

The page also includes tips on how to choose a program and what sorts of financial aid opportunities exist.

The library schools in the following list now offer degree programs online,[11] although some may have limited course selections in all-online format, and some require brief mandatory on-campus residencies. These conditions can change quickly, so be sure to check the school's Web site to find out what the current online options are.

University of Alabama School of Library & Information Studies
http://www.slis.ua.edu/mlis/index.html
Requires 4-day orientation course

University of Arizona School of Information Resources & Library Science
http://www.sir.arizona.edu/program/masters/distanceIntro.htm
Requires 7-day orientation course

Clarion University Department of Library Science
http://www.clarion.edu/libsci/

Drexel University College of Information Science & Technology
http://www.drexel.com/online-degrees/information-sciences-degrees/ms-di/index.
    aspx

The Florida State University College of Information
http://ci.fsu.edu/go/graduate/online_degrees_grad

University of Illinois at Urbana-Champaign Graduate School of Library and Information Science
http://www.lis.uiuc.edu/programs/leep/
Requires brief on-campus sessions

North Carolina Central University School of Library and Information Sciences
http://www.nccuslis.org/distancelearning/dlearn_int.php

University of North Texas School of Library & Information Sciences
http://www.unt.edu/slis/viatheweb/viaweb.htm
Requires 8- or 9-day residency

University of Pittsburgh School of Information Sciences
http://fasttrack.sis.pitt.edu/
Requires 5-day orientation + 1 weekend and 1 term

Rutgers School of Communication, Information and Library Studies
http://www.scils.rutgers.edu/programs/lis/OnlineMLIS.jsp
(for School Library Media & Digital Libraries concentrations only).
Requires 2 days orientation + 1 optional day per year

San José State University School of Library and Information Science
http://slisweb.sjsu.edu/slis/disted.htm

University of South Carolina
http://www.libsci.sc.edu/de/

University of South Florida School of Library & Information Sciences
http://www.cas.usf.edu/lis/
Requires 2 face-to-face courses

Southern Connecticut State University Department of Information & Library Science
http://www.southernct.edu/departments/ils/

University of Southern Mississippi School of Library & Information Science
http://www.usm.edu/slis/distlearn.htm

Syracuse University School of Information Studies
http://ischool.syr.edu/academics/distance/index.asp
Requires 7-day residency

University of Tennessee School of Information Sciences
http://www.sis.utk.edu/programs/distance
Requires 2-day orientation

Texas Women's University School of Library & Information Studies
http://www.twu.edu/cope/slis/disted.htm

University of Washington Information School
http://www.ischool.washington.edu/mlis/
Requires 3–5 day residency each quarter

University of Wisconsin-Milwaukee School of Information Studies
http://www.uwm.edu/Dept/SOIS/academics/DE/

IN SUM

Reference work is very public work. It places you at the center of the community; people will come to trust your work and rely on your skills. Establishing and maintaining good connections with your patrons, your library board, and other local officials are, of course, essential parts of your job. To keep your knowledge, your abilities, and your library's resources up to date, it's equally important that you interact with others in the library profession, calling on them when you need to, and helping them out when you can. By taking full advantage of what your state and local library systems have to offer, participating in professional associations, staying on top of new developments and new ideas, and challenging yourself to learn as much as you can about the profession, you'll be in a wonderful position to respond fully to the needs of the people in your community.

REVIEW

1. Explore the Web sites for your state library and state library association. Can you find information about one training or continuing education opportunity, one potential source of funding, an upcoming statewide conference, and one listserv or electronic newsletter you might like to subscribe to?

2. Locate an archived video or audio seminar on an interesting topic and watch or listen to it. Did you learn anything you can apply in your work? Would it be worthwhile to access more of these materials, and can you make time to do so?

3. Subscribe to at least one of the e-mail discussion lists and at least two of the RSS feeds mentioned in this chapter. After a couple of weeks, evaluate: are these good methods for keeping informed on reference issues on a day-to-day basis?

NOTES

1. Rosser-Hogben, D.M. (2004). Meeting the challenge: An overview of the information needs of rural America. *Rural Libraries, 24* (1), 25–49.
2. Bushing, M.C. (1995). *The professionalization of rural librarians: Role modeling, networking, and continuing education* [Doctoral dissertation]. Bozeman, MT: Montana State University—Bozeman.
3. Gervasi, A., & Seibt, B.K. (1988). *Handbook for small, rural, and emerging public libraries.* Phoenix: Oryx Press, p. 7.
4. Heuertz, L., Gordon, A.C., Gordon, M.T., Moore, E.J. (2003). The impact of public access computing on rural and small town libraries. *Rural Libraries, 23* (1), 51–79; Kline, K.A. (2002). Libraries, schools, and wired communities in rural areas and the changing communications landscape. *Rural Libraries, 22* (2), 13–41.
5. Boris, L. (2005). The digital divide and its impact on the rural community. *Rural Libraries, 25* (2), 7–35.
6. Gervasi & Seibt, *Handbook for small, rural*; Vavrek, B. (1995). *Rural and small libraries: Providers for lifelong learning.* ERIC Document 385254; Bertot, J.C., McClure, C.R., Jaeger, P.T., & Ryan, J. *Public libraries and the Internet 2006: Study results and findings.* Prepared for the Bill and Melinda Gates Foundation and the American Library Association. Tallahassee: Florida State University Information Use Management and Policy Institute. Available online at http://www.ii.fsu.edu/plinternet_reports.cfm
7. Bertot et al., *Public Libraries.* For examples of state libraries where each of these services is in place see http://www.ii.fsu.edu/projectFiles/plinternet/2006/Appendix8.pdf
8. A nice synopsis of support appears in Linda Fox's (1999) *The volunteer library: A handbook* (Jefferson, NC: McFarland), part 6.
9. American Library Association (2007). Available online at http://www.ala.org
10. Bernard Vavrek, personal communication, June 29, 2007.
11. Data is from Central Jersey Regional Library Cooperative (2001–2007). Distance Ed Comparison. Retrieved from the Become a Librarian! Web site at http://www.becomea librarian.org/DistanceEdComparison.htm

CHAPTER 12

For More Information

A journey of a thousand miles begins with a single step.[1]

Your journey into the world of reference has only just begun. I hope this brief introduction to some of the services and sources you can offer your patrons has proven useful, but I know you will want to spend more time exploring those topics and issues that caught your interest. This chapter pulls together full references for some of the more useful sources mentioned throughout the book. If you have suggestions for additional resources you would like to see included here, please let me know. Sharing our knowledge and our ideas is the best way to advance our understanding of reference and to offer the best possible service to our patrons. Please feel free to contact me if I can be of assistance to you: cford@slis.sjsu.edu.

Happy trails!

GENERAL SOURCES ABOUT REFERENCE SERVICE (CHAPTER 1)

Green, S.S. (1876). Personal relations between librarians and readers. *Library Journal, 1*, 74–81. Available online at http://polaris.gseis.ucla.edu/jrichardson/DIS220/personal. htm. This important article marks the birth of reference librarianship.

Each of the following three textbooks provides a thorough introduction to reference sources and the provision of reference services:

Bopp, R. E., & Smith, L. C. (Eds.). (2001). *Reference and information services: An introduction* (3rd ed.). Englewood, CO: Libraries Unlimited (4th edition due out in 2008).

Cassell, K. A., & Hiremath, U. (2006). *Reference and information services in the 21st century: An introduction.* New York: Neal-Schuman Publishers.

Katz, W. A. (2002). *Introduction to reference work* (8th ed.). Boston: McGraw-Hill.

A highly readable discussion of some of the changes occurring in reference work may be found in:

Janes, J. (2003). *Introduction to reference work in the digital age.* New York: Neal-Schuman.

THE REFERENCE INTERVIEW AND INTERPERSONAL COMMUNICATION (CHAPTER 2)

Reference & User Services Association. Guidelines for Behavioral Performance of Reference and Information Service Providers. Available at: http://www.ala.org/ala/rusa/ protools/referenceguide/guidelinesbehavioral.cfm. These guidelines set the professional standard for effective reference interviewing skills.

Ross, C. S., Nilsen, K., & Dewdney, P. (2002). *Conducting the reference interview: A how-to-do-it manual for librarians.* New York: Neal-Schuman. A practical manual for the working professional.

Some excellent online tutorials and practical tips are available at:

ORE Ohio Reference Excellence on the Web (Ohio Library Council). http://www.olc.org/ ore/

Reference 123 Training for Libraries (Houston Area Library System). http://www.hals.lib. tx.us/ref123/

STAR Reference Manual (Nebraska Library Commission). http://www.nlc.state.ne.us/ref/ star/star.html

ALA's Reference & User Services Association (RUSA) also offers an ongoing series of Web-based, instructor-led professional development courses covering reference, readers' advisory, and marketing. See:

RUSA Professional Development Online. http://www.ala.org/ala/rusa/rusaevents/professionaldevelopmentonline/prodevonline.cfm

BUILDING AND MAINTAINING A QUALITY REFERENCE COLLECTION (CHAPTER 3)

Two good general introductions to collection development basics are:

Evans, G. E., & Saponaro, M. Z. (2005). *Developing library and information center collections* (5th ed.). Westport, CT: Libraries Unlimited.

Johnson, P. (2004). *Fundamentals of collection development & management.* Chicago: American Library Association.

The following source deals specifically with developing the reference collection:

Reference collection development: A manual (2nd. ed.) (2004). Chicago: Reference and User Services Association, American Library Association.

Selection aids for smaller libraries mentioned include:

Graff Hysell, S. *Recommended reference books for small and medium-sized libraries and media centers.* Littleton, CO: Libraries Unlimited (a subset of books appearing in ARBA, compiled annually).

Lewis, A. (1998) *Madame Audrey's guide to mostly cheap but good reference books for small and rural libraries.* Chicago: American Library Association.

O'Gorman, J. (Ed). (2007). *Reference sources for small and medium-sized libraries* (7th ed). Chicago: American Library Association.

Sweetland, J.H. (2001). *Fundamental reference sources.* Chicago: American Library Association.

The Alabama Library Association's suggested basic reference collection is available online at the Alabama Public Library Service's Web site:

Alabama Library Association Standards Committee. *Suggestions for a basic reference collection.* http://www.apls.state.al.us/webpages/pubs/standardsbasicrefcoll.pdf

Each of these periodicals includes reviews of reference sources, as well as other sources:

Booklist
American Libraries (May issue covers "best reference sources")
Library Journal (April 15 issue covers "best reference sources")

Checklists of evaluation criteria mentioned include:

Beck, S.E. *The good, the bad & the ugly: Or, why it's a good idea to evaluate Web sources.* (1997). Available online at the New Mexico State University Library Web site: http://lib.nmsu.edu/instruction/eval.html

Critical evaluation of resources (2007). Available online at the University of California, Berkeley Teaching Library Web site: http://www.lib.berkeley.edu/TeachingLib/Guides/Evaluation.html

Critically analyzing information sources. (2004). Available online at the Cornell University Library Web site: http://www.library.cornell.edu/olinuris/ref/research/skill26.htm

ONLINE SEARCHING (CHAPTER 4)

Bolner, M.S., and Poirier, G.A. (2007). *The research process: books & beyond* (4th ed). Dubuque, IA: Kendall/Hunt. A useful treatment of many aspects of research, aimed at undergraduate students. Chapter 3 covers searching online databases;

Chapter 5 discusses searching the Internet; and Chapter 7 includes a good current listing of basic reference sources.

Notess, G.R. (2006). *Search Engine Features.* Available online at http://searchengine showdown.com/features/. A handy comparative chart.

Sullivan, Danny. *How search engines work.* (2007, March 14). Available online at http://searchenginewatch.com/showPage.html?page=2168031. A clear explanation of how search engines function.

Walker, G. & Janes, J. (1999). *Online retrieval: A dialogue of theory and practice.* Englewood, CO: Libraries Unlimited. Although the Walker & Janes book is somewhat dated, it explains database structure very clearly, and the authors do an excellent job of laying out the steps in online searching (in Chapter 6).

Many libraries have developed online information literacy tutorials that aim to teach selection, evaluation, and searching skills. Some premier examples:

Kentucky Virtual Library's *How to do research* (for children) http://www.kyvl.org/html/kids/homebase.html

Ohio State University's *net.TUTOR* http://gateway.lib.ohio-state.edu/tutor

University of Texas's *Texas Information Literacy Tutorial: TILT* http://tilt.lib.utsystem.edu/

Web Search Engines Mentioned in Chapter 4

Keyword search engines:
Ask.com http://ask.com
Google http://www.google.com
Live Search http://www.live.com
Yahoo! http://www.yahoo.com

Meta-search engines:
Clusty http://clusty.com
Dogpile http://www.dogpile.com
Kartoo http://www.kartoo.com
Mamma http://www.mamma.com

Subject search engines:
Findlaw http://www.findlaw.com
Scirus http://www.scirus.com
Usa.gov http://www.usa.gov

Directories:
Infomine http://infomine.ucr.edu
Open Directory Project http://dmoz.org
Yahoo! Directory http://dir.yahoo.com

LIBRARY CATALOGS AND BIBLIOGRAPHIES (CHAPTER 5)

Sources to consider include:

Amazon.com http://www.amazon.com
Bibliographic Index (H. W. Wilson) http://www.hwwilson.com
Books in Print (R. R. Bowker) http://booksinprint.com
OCLC WorldCat http://www.worldcat.org (or by subscription: http://firstsearch.
   oclc.org)
Library of Congress catalog http://catalog.loc.gov/
Your own library catalog
Your state union catalog (if one is available)

INDEXES AND DATABASES (CHAPTER 6)

As a reminder, the major commercial publishers mentioned in Chapter 6 are EBSCO (http://www.ebsco.com), Gale (http://gale.cengage.com), LexisNexis (http://www.lexisnexis.com), OCLC (http://www.oclc.org), ProQuest (http://www.proquest.com), and H. W. Wilson (http://www.hwwilson.com). Important sources to consider include:

General

Academic Search Premier (EBSCO)
Expanded Academic ASAP (Gale)
Google Scholar http://scholar.google.com
Infotrac OneFile (Gale)
LexisNexis Academic (Lexis Nexis)
Live Search Academic http://academic.live.com
ProQuest Research Library (ProQuest)
Reader's Guide to Periodical Literature (H. W. Wilson)

Newspapers

Google News Archive Search http://news.google.com/archivesearch
LexisNexis Academic (Lexis Nexis)
National Newspaper Index (Gale)
New York Times http://www.nytimes.com

Newspaper Source (EBSCO)
OnlineNewspapers.com http://onlinenewspapers.com
ProQuest Newsstand (ProQuest)
SmallTownPapers http://SmallTownPapers.com.

Specialized Indexes

By Age Groups

Infotrac Kids and *InfoTrac Junior Edition* (Gale)
Primary Search and *Middle Search Plus* (EBSCO)
Student Resource Center (Gale)

By Genre

Biography Index (H.W. Wilson)
Play Index (H.W. Wilson)
Short Story Index (H.W. Wilson)

By Subject Area

Education Resource Information Center (ERIC) (U.S. Department of Education)
    http://eric.ed.gov
LegalTrac (Gale)
PsycInfo (American Psychological Association)
PubMed (U.S. National Library of Medicine) http://www.pubmed.gov

H.W. Wilson subject indexes:
Education Full Text
General Science Full Text
Humanities Full Text
Social Sciences Full Text
Wilson Business Full Text

Aggregated Databases

Business & Company Resource Center (Gale)
Business Source Premier (EBSCO)
Literature Resource Center (Gale)
Health & Wellness Resource Center (Gale)
SIRS Knowledge Source (ProQuest)

Serials Control

EBSCO A to Z http://www.ebsco.com/atoz/
Serials Solutions http://www.serialssolutions.com
Ulrich's Periodicals Directory http://ulrichsweb.com

ENCYCLOPEDIAS AND DICTIONARIES (CHAPTER 7)

Sources to consider include:

For Adults

Columbia Encyclopedia (a one volume work in its print version) http://www. infoplease.com/encyclopedia/
Encyclopedia Americana http://go.grolier.com
Encyclopaedia Britannica and *Britannica Online* http://www.britannica.com
MSN Encarta http://encarta.msn.com
Wikipedia http://www.wikipedia.org

For Young Adults and Children

Compton's Encyclopedia (Britannica) http://www.britannica.com
The New Book of Knowledge (Grolier) http://go.grolier.com
World Book Encyclopedia http://www.worldbook.com

Unabridged Dictionaries

Oxford English Dictionary http://www.oed.com (by subscription)
Random House Webster's Unabridged Dictionary (free subset available at http://www.infoplease.com/dictionary.html)
Webster's Third New International Dictionary http://www.merriam-websterunabridged.com (by subscription)

Abridged Dictionaries

The American Heritage Dictionary, 4th ed. http://www.bartleby.com/61/
Merriam-Webster's Collegiate Dictionary (by subscription at http://www.merriam-webstercollegiate.com; free subset available at http://www.m-w.com)

Dictionaries for Children

Macmillan *Dictionary for Children* and *Dictionary for Students*
Merriam-Webster free online dictionary http://wordcentral.com
Thorndike-Barnhart *Children's Dictionary, Junior Dictionary,* and *Student Dictionary*

Useful Free Online Sources

Dictionary.com http://dictionary.com
ForeignWord.com http://foreignword.com
One Look Dictionary Search http://onelook.com
Word2Word Language Resources http://www.word2word.com

Thesauri

Merriam Webster Thesaurus http://www.m-w.com
Roget's International Thesaurus http://www.bartleby.com/thesauri (1922 and
   1995 versions)
Roget's College Thesaurus in Dictionary Form (Penguin; Signet)

READY REFERENCE SOURCES (CHAPTER 8)

Sources to consider include:

Almanacs

Time Almanac (formerly Information Please Almanac) http://www.infoplease.com
World Almanac and Book of Facts (World Almanac Books)

Directories

Anywho http://anywho.com
Switchboard http://switchboard.com

Quotation Sources

Bartlett's Familiar Quotations http://bartleby.com/100/
Columbia World of Quotations http://bartleby.com/66/
Respectfully Quoted: A Dictionary of Quotations http://bartleby.com/73/
Simpson's Contemporary Quotations http://bartleby.com/63/

Handbooks, Manuals, Guides

Merck Manual of Diagnosis & Therapy http://www.merck.com/mmpe/
Occupational Outlook Handbook http://www.bls.gov/oco/

Sources of Country Information

CIA WorldZ Factbook https://www.cia.gov/library/publications/the-world-factbook/
Statesman's Yearbook http://www.statesmansyearbook.com (by subscription)

Chronologies

Chase's Calendar of Events (McGraw-Hill)
Timetables of History, 3rd ed. (Simon & Schuster/Touchstone)

Statistical Sources

Statistical Abstract http://www.census.gov/compendia/statab/
U.S. Census Bureau Web site, including *American FactFinder* http://www.census.gov

FREE WEB SOURCES (CHAPTER 9)

Sources to consider include:

ALA Best Free Reference Web Sites (1999–present) http://www.ala.org/ala/rusa/rusaourassoc/rusasections/mars/marspubs/MARSBESTIndex.htm

BUBL LINK Catalogue of Internet Sources: Reference http://bubl.ac.uk/link/r/reference.htm

Internet Public Library: Reference http://www.ipl.org/div/subject/browse/ref00.00.00

Librarians' Internet Index: Ready Reference and Quick Facts http://search.lii.org/index.jsp?more=SubTopic10

Library of Congress Virtual Reference Shelf http://www.loc.gov/rr/askalib/virtualref.html

LibrarySpot http://www.libraryspot.com

Refdesk.com: Reference Desk http://refdesk.com/refdsk.html

This bibliography may also be helpful:

Morse, L. (2006). 100 best free reference Web sites. *The Reference Librarian, 44,* 279–95.

Current Awareness Sources

Gary Price's Resource Shelf http://www.resourceshelf.com

Internet Scout Project's *Scout Report* http://scout.wisc.edu/About/subscribe.php

Librarians' Internet Index "New This Week" http://lii.org/pub/htdocs/subscribe.htm

Developing Web Pages

Krug, S. (2006). *Don't make me think! A common sense approach to Web usability* (2nd edition). Berkeley, CA: New Riders.

Mercado, A. (2003). Public library research link collections. *Public Libraries, 42,* 360–361. Available online at http://www.ala.org/ala/pla/plapubs/publiclibraries/42n6.pdf

Nielsen, J. Top Ten Guidelines for Homepage Usability and Top Ten Web Design Mistakes http://www.useit.com/alertbox/20020512.html http://www.useit.com/alertbox/designmistakes.html

United States Department of Health & Human Services (2006). Research-based Web Design & Usability Guidelines. Available at http://www.usability.gov/pdfs/guidelines.html

Chat and Instant Message Reference Service

OCLC QuestionPoint http://www.questionpoint.org

Tutor.com Ask a Librarian http://www.tutor.com

Houghton, S., & Schmidt, A. (2005). Web-based chat vs. instant messaging: Who wins? *Online, 29* (4), 26–30

Schmidt, A., & Stephens, M. (2005). IM me. *Library Journal, 130,* 34–35.

PROFESSIONAL ETHICS AND POLICY DEVELOPMENT (CHAPTER 10)

American Library Association Documents

ALA Code of Ethics (1995). http://www.ala.org/ala/oif/statementspols/codeofethics/codeethics.htm

ALA Core Values Statement (2004). http://www.ala.org/ala/oif/statementspols/corevaluesstatement/corevalues.htm

ALA Library Bill of Rights (1996). http://www.ala.org/ala/oif/statementspols/statementsif/librarybillrights.htm

Filters and Filtering (2007). http://www.ala.org/ala/oif/ifissues/filtersfiltering.htm

Reference & User Services Association (2001). Guidelines for Medical, Legal, and Business Responses. http://www.ala.org/ala/rusa/protools/referenceguide/guidelinesmedical.cfm

General Ethical Considerations

Bunge, C.A. (1999/1990). Ethics and the reference librarian. *The Reference Librarian, 66,* 25–43.

Dowd, R.C. (1989). I want to find out how to freebase cocaine, or yet another unobtrusive test of reference performance. *The Reference Librarian, 25/26,* 483–93.

Hauptman, R. (1976). Professionalism or culpability? An experiment in ethics. *Wilson Library Bulletin, 50,* 626–27.

Swan, J.C. (1982). Ethics at the reference desk: Comfortable theories and tricky practices. *The Reference Librarian, 4,* 99–121.

Copyright Information

U.S. Copyright Office (2006). Circular 1: Copyright Office Basics. http://www.copyright.gov/circs/circ1.html

U.S. Copyright Office (2006). FL-102: Fair Use. http://www.copyright.gov/fls/fl102.html

Stanford University Libraries (2004). Copyright and Fair Use. http://fairuse.stanford.edu/Copyright_and_Fair_Use_Overview

Crews, K.D. (2006). *Copyright law for librarians and educators: Creative strategies and practical solutions* (2nd ed). Chicago: American Library Association.

Library Policies

Brumley, R. (2006). *The reference librarian's policies, forms, guidelines, and procedures handbook: With CD-ROM.* New York: Neal-Schuman Publishers.

Nelson, S.S., & Garcia, J. (2003). *Creating policies for results: From chaos to clarity.* Chicago: American Library Association.

Wood, R.J., & Hoffmann, F.W. (2005). *Library collection development policies: Academic, public, and special libraries.* Lanham, MD: Scarecrow Press.

Sample Library Policies on the Web

American Library Association Intellectual Freedom Statements and Policies http://www.ala.org/ala/oif/statementspols/statementspolicies.htm

MGPL Webrary Collection Development Policy (Morton Grove Public Library, IL) http://www.webrary.org/inside/colldevadultref.html

OwlsWeb Links for Libraries (Outagamie Waupaca Library System, Wisconsin) http://www.owlsweb.info/L4L/policies.asp

State Library of Ohio Sample Library Policy Statements http://winslo.state.oh.us/publib/policies.html

PROFESSIONAL NETWORKING AND CONTINUING EDUCATION (CHAPTER 11)

Association Web Sites

ALA Events & Conferences page http://www.ala.org/ala/events/eventsconferences.htm

American Library Association http://www.ala.org/

Association of Rural and Small Libraries (ARSL) http://arsl.clarion.edu/

Committee on Rural, Native and Tribal Libraries http://www.ala.org/Rural Libraries

COSLA Profiles of State Library Agencies http://www.cosla.org/profiles/ (includes links to state library homepages, state library associations, and state virtual libraries.)

LSSIRT—Library Support Staff Interests Round Table http://www.ala.org/ala/lssirt/lssirt.htm

PLA—Public Library Association http://www.ala.org/pla

RUSA—Reference & User Services Association http://www.ala.org/rusa

WebJunction http://www.webjunction.org

Journals

American Libraries http://www.ala.org/ala/alonline/

Library Journal http://www.libraryjournal.com/

The Reference Librarian (available online through Haworth Press)

Reference Services Review (available online through Emerald Journals)

Reference & User Services Quarterly (RUSQ) http://www.rusq.org

Rural Libraries http://jupiter.clarion.edu/~csrl/rural.htm

Listservs

LIBREF-L http://listserv.kent.edu/scripts/wa.exe?SUBED1=libref-l&A=1

Project Wombat http://lists.project-wombat.org

PUBLIB http://lists.webjunction.org/publib/

Blogs

Public Library Association http://www.plablog.org

Reference and User Services Association http://www.rusablog.org

ResourceShelf http://www.resourceshelf.com

WebJunction http://blog.webjunctionworks.org/

Continuing Education

ALA Continuing Education page http://www.ala.org/ala/education/ce/continuingeducation.htm

Education Institute http://www.thepartnership.ca/partnership/bins/index_ei.asp?cid=83&lang=1

InfoPeople training materials http://www.infopeople.org/training/past/

SirsiDynix Institute http://www.sirsidynixinstitute.com

WebJunction E-learning clearinghouse http://www.webjunction.org/do/DisplayContent?id=13651

Master's Degree Programs in Librarianship

ALA Directory of Institutions Offering ALA-Accredited Master's Programs in Library and Information Studies (2007). http://www.ala.org/ala/accreditation/lisdirb/lisdirectory.htm

ALA Education & Careers page (2007). http://www.ala.org/ala/education/degrees/degrees.htm

Central Jersey Regional Library Cooperative (2001–2007). *Distance Ed Comparison.* Retrieved from the Become a Librarian! Web site at http://www.becomealibrarian.org/DistanceEdComparison.htm

Publications of General Interest

Fox, L. (1999). *The volunteer library: A handbook.* Jefferson, NC: McFarland. Includes useful information on networking in the profession.

Gervasi, A., & Seibt, B. K. (1988). *Handbook for small, rural, and emerging public libraries.* Phoenix: Oryx Press. Now dated, but full of good ideas about networking in the community.

Siess, J. A. (2006). *The new OPL sourcebook: A guide for solo and small libraries.* Medford, NJ: Information Today. (There is also an OPL Newsletter available for subscription at http://www.ibi-opl.com/newsletter/index.html)

NOTE

1.   Chinese proverb (attributed to Lao-tzu). *The Columbia World of Quotations* (1996). Available online at http://www.bartleby.com/66/73/1873.html.

INDEX

ABOUT THE AUTHOR

CHARLOTTE FORD is an assistant professor in the School of Library and Information Science at San José State University. She holds a B.A. from Earlham College and M.L.S. and Ph.D. degrees from Indiana University. She has worked as a reference librarian in Miami, Florida; Bogotá, Colombia; and Birmingham, Alabama.